The Union Member's Complete Guide

Also published by Union Communication Services, Inc.

The Union Steward's Complete Guide
Edited by David Prosten

The Union Member's Complete Guide

EVERYTHING YOU WANT—AND *NEED*—TO KNOW ABOUT WORKING UNION

By Michael Mauer

Union Communication Services, Inc.
Annapolis, Maryland

Grateful acknowledgment to Pete Seeger for permission to quote from his "Talking Union."

Library of Congress Control Number: 2001095173
ISBN: 0-9659486-1-7

Michael Mauer is a member of the National Writers Union, UAW Local 1981.

Design and typesetting by Gerson Higgs Design, Washington, D.C. Carol Higgs is a member of Columbia Typographical Union No. 101-12 of Communications Workers of America.

Illustrations by Kelley Bell.

Printed in the United States of America by members of GCIU Local 144-B at McArdle Printing Company. Printed on Cougar Text paper made by members of the Paper, Allied-Industrial, Chemical Employees (PACE) and the United Auto Workers (UAW).

0 9 8 7 6 5 4 3 2 1

In loving memory of my father, who revealed to me nearly everything about human decency—the sanctity of picket lines, and a helluva lot more—in what seemed like an instant.

It must have been something to have been Joe Mauer.

Acknowledgments   ix

Introduction   1

CHAPTER 1   **What Are Unions?**   5

CHAPTER 2   **How Your Union Operates**   13

CHAPTER 3   **A Member's Rights and Responsibilities**   23

CHAPTER 4   **The Union's Responsibility to Its Members**   33

CHAPTER 5   **Your Union Contract: Getting There**   41

CHAPTER 6   **Your Union Contract: What It Covers**   57

CHAPTER 7   **Grievances: Enforcing Workplace Law**   67

CHAPTER 8   **Arbitration: The End of the Line**   79

CHAPTER 9   **Where Do Workplace Rights Come From?**   87

CHAPTER 10 **If You Get in Trouble . . .**   103

CHAPTER 11 **The Union's Face Outside the Workplace**   109

CHAPTER 12 **Your Role in Your Union**   117

            Glossary   125

            Helpful Contacts   133

            Directory of Unions   139

            Index   151

ACKNOWLEDGMENTS

If this book renders a service to the union movement, thanks are due to David Prosten, who saw a need and decided to fill it. His encouragement as an editor and scrupulously fair dealings as a publisher showed me what a valuable part of the labor movement he is, and what a fine human being, too.

The wisdom of selecting me to undertake the task of writing this book remains to be seen. But it certainly has been personally fulfilling. I knew there must be some reason I'd chosen to perform such a wide range of union work—beginning as a lawyer with the National Labor Relations Board, then moving on to lawyering, bargaining, and organizing with unions representing so many different types of public and private sector workers: the American Federation of State, County and Municipal Employees, the National Education Association, the National Treasury Employees Union, the Newspaper Guild, and the Service Employees International Union—before arriving at my present post with the American Association of University Professors. I like to think my breadth of experience in the labor movement prepared me for this task.

When David first approached me with the book idea, I didn't realize how totally unnecessary it would be to arm myself to negotiate a fair book contract. So I did what every worker should do before dealing with the boss: I consulted with my union rep. In this case, that meant contacting Phil Mattera of the National Writers Union, UAW Local 1981. For his time, wisdom and (as it turned out, unnecessary!) advice, I'm appreciative.

I've had the privilege of working with a lot of smart and dedicated union activists, and I'm grateful to all who taught me through the years. To three who were kind enough to review my manuscript and to help me improve it, I offer special thanks: my AAUP colleagues Ernie Benjamin and Pat Shaw, and Jeff Lustig, professor at Cal State–Sacramento and activist in his union, the California Faculty Association. Sarah Flynn's assistance throughout the development of this book greatly improved the final product. To the readers, I assure you that whatever errors of commission, omission, fact or presentation that appear here are my responsibility alone.

Like most of us in the union movement, I've gotten the motivation and inspiration needed to fight the good fight from a number of different sources. For nearly three decades, my thinking and my actions have been shaped in great measure by two invaluable lessons: that limits are not ascertainable and truths not readily apparent. For holding the doors open for me over the years, I offer gratitude to my shotokan karate teachers, most particularly Masataka Mori Sensei.

Finally, the family environment I grew up in and the one I'm fortunate enough to have now have given me what I needed to keep plugging away till this book was completed. So my gratitude, in large doses, extends to my mom, Millie Mauer (who showed me early on, by example, that the perceived limits are not the real ones), and to Marc Mauer, who's never stopped being my inspirational big brother. And I can't summon the words to convey my love and admiration for Jan Fritz, my best friend and wife, and for Jossi and Matthew Fritz-Mauer, the two greatest guys that ever were.

The Union Member's Complete Guide

INTRODUCTION

If you're reading this book, odds are you're working in a union-ized workplace—not because you participated in an organizing drive, but rather because your new workplace had unionized long ago. While organizing drives take place every day of the year, all over the country, the overwhelming majority of Americans who are represented by a union—probably well over 95 percent—did not personally participate in the effort. That job was undertaken by the workers who preceded them. Since you may have "inherited" a union, you're not entirely clear about what that means. You want a better understanding of how your union works, your rights as a member, and your duties as one. You might not be convinced that you're stronger because of your union, or that as just one person you can do things that will build the union's strength or have an impact on the way the union operates.

On the other hand, maybe you're reading this book because you're employed in a non-union workplace, and you're curious about what life would be like if you and your co-workers had union representation. Although this book speaks directly to unionized workers, it paints a pretty good picture of what to expect if you and your co-workers "go union."

Or maybe you're one of those people who has just gone through a successful union organizing drive. Your entire workplace is on the verge of making the change to a union environment. You'd like a roadmap of what's next.

No matter. For all readers, this book steps back a pace and talks about the fundamentals of unionism. We'll examine the basic elements of what a union does, how it does it, and your role in it all, so that you'll better understand how working life is improved when you have union representation. And you'll learn what you can—and should—do to make your voice heard when your union makes decisions that will affect you.

Why learn about unions? Because unions change nearly every aspect of workplace life.

◆ Starting on a very practical level, everyone in a unionized workplace gets to make a decision as to whether to be a full, dues-paying member. You'll want to understand what unions do and how you fit into the picture, to make the smart decision: to become a full, active and involved member.

◆ You can't know where you're going if you don't understand where you've been. Things are the way they are in your workplace and others because millions of workers won the fight to be represented by unions. The modern American labor movement has transformed tens of thousands of workplaces, and tens of millions of lives. Unionized workers earn more money, enjoy more benefits, and have greater job security than their non-union counterparts. (And, as you'll see later on, even non-union workers' jobs are improved because so many other workers have unionized.)

◆ If you're like every other person who's ever lived, it's probably fair to say that there are some aspects of your working life that you don't like. Because unions are the most powerful tool workers have to gain control over what goes on in the workplace, to improve your situation you need to understand the possibilities and limitations of what a union can do.

◆ The labor movement has been a major force in shaping American society. When you're a union member, and when you become actively involved in all the things the union does, you become part of something bigger than your individual life, and bigger than your workplace: you become part of one of the largest social movements in America today, a movement of close to 17 million men and women.

◆ Finally, the fate of unionized American workers more and more is linked to the fortune of our fellow workers the world over. So American unions are speaking up more and more on international trade and environmental issues, human rights standards, and just about every other global issue. If your employer can get away with having a Mexican worker produce what you produce, at a fraction of your pay and no benefits, you better believe he'll do it. And he won't much care if a few rivers end up flowing with cancer-causing toxins in the process, either.

A Note About the Scope of This Book

People come in all shapes and sizes, and so do labor unions. There are public sector unions, representing employees of governments at all levels, and private sector unions, representing workers at privately owned companies. There are unionized workplaces in states, cities and towns with labor friendly laws, and there are unions in workplaces and locations where employees don't even have a legally protected right to bargain a contract. Different unions have dramatically different ways of structuring themselves and making decisions.

But no matter what setting you're in, there are basic concepts of labor-management relations, and the role of unions, that apply. So this book can give you a working knowledge of the nuts and bolts of union representation. As you read, though, keep in mind that the way things operate where you work will vary depending on what union you are represented by, what type of work you do, and a lot more. For specific answers to many questions that come up in your workplace, you'll need to consult with your union, with a knowledgeable lawyer, with an appropriate government agency, or with a worker advocacy group.

WHAT ARE

unions?

A union is nothing more complicated than a group of workers who have chosen to band together to promote their common interests. One person standing alone may be weak, but many joined together are powerful.

This very basic understanding has been expressed over the years by all kinds of people in all kinds of ways. Chief Justice Charles Evans Hughes put it this way in a 1937 United States Supreme Court decision: "Long ago we stated the reason for labor organizations. We said that they were organized out of the necessities of the situation; that a single employee was helpless in dealing with an employer . . . that union was essential to give laborers opportunity to deal on an equal [basis] with their employer."

Pretty much the same sentiment was expressed very differently just a few years later in song by folk singer and activist Pete Seeger:

You got a union now and you're sitting pretty;
Put some of the boys on the steering committee.
The boss won't listen when one guy squawks
But he's got to listen when the union talks.
He'd better . . . he'll be mighty lonely . . .
If everybody decided to walk out on him.

So that's the basic concept: in unity there is strength. But to understand more fully what unions are all about, let's take a look at how having a union changes some of the basic organization of a workplace and the relationship of the people within the workplace.

Workplace Structure: Union and Non-Union

The structure and the power relationships of a workplace where there is no union are very different from those in a unionized facility. In the non-union workplace, employees are simply a collection of individuals, organized into groups according to the employer's needs. Workers are categorized based on what type of work you do, the location in which you perform your work, the shift you may happen to work on, or other factors relating to the ways in which the employer chooses to get the work done. Some employers deliberately structure the work and the workplace precisely to discourage the unionization of their employees.

The employees' role in a unionized workplace is quite different. With a union, those who work for a particular employer are no longer just a bunch of individuals; they are a collective unit, as well. The union has the right— and the legal obligation—to speak with one voice, on behalf of all of the employees in what is known as the "bargaining unit." This means that the employer loses the power advantage of dealing only with individuals, one-on-one. With union representation in place, the employer has to reckon with the union as the collective voice of all of the union-represented workers.

A Difficult Balancing Act

Of course, there's a tradeoff involved here. You, as an individual, gain strength by uniting through the union with others in your workplace. Using your collective power you have greater strength to defend and promote your interests, like higher pay and better benefits. But as in any democracy, when we make decisions and act as a group we lose a little bit of individual control. For the good of the group, each individual necessarily gives up a bit of the ability to do whatever he or she pleases. You may, for example, enjoy the good company and the activities that come from being a member of a

Moose lodge or a church or community group. But you also understand that your membership obligates you to live by certain rules of the organization and to make some financial contributions. It's the same with being a member of a union: you get the good things that come from being part of a group, but you have to give up a certain amount of individual control. (As you think about that, though, don't forget this: in a non-union workplace the employer makes *all* the rules.)

What can sometimes make life in a union tricky to deal with is that the group of union members does not consist of people with 100 percent identical interests and needs. Within any group, there are some things that everyone has in common (like everyone in your union working for the same employer), but also other things that are different (like night shift workers wanting extra pay for working at night, or day workers needing better parking). Or sometimes only one employee has a workplace problem requiring union help, such as fighting a disciplinary action. But even though it's just one person, the union must still advocate for that individual. And the union's voice must be heard, as well, for all the different smaller groups of employees

WORKING NON-UNION VS. WORKING UNION

◆ In a non-union setting, workers count on their own individual strength; in a union setting, workers count on their own strength plus the collective strength of the group.

◆ In a non-union setting, the employer makes all the rules; in a union setting, the rules are negotiated by the union and the employer.

◆ In a non-union setting, the employer enforces the rules however he sees fit; in a union setting workers have a procedure in place to respond to unfair enforcement of rules, even to the point of having an outside, neutral arbitrator decide who's right.

◆ In a non-union setting the employer decides what employees will be paid and what benefits, if any, they will receive; in a union setting the employer is required to negotiate with the union on all pay and benefit issues the union brings to the bargaining table.

in the workplace, whether those groupings are based on shift, work classification, age, how much money people earn, or any other employment-related factors.

As you can imagine, for the union to make decisions, it can get a little complicated. It's not uncommon to have situations where individuals or smaller groups within the bargaining unit have potentially conflicting interests. Example: two union-represented employees get into a fight. Each claims that the other started the fight. It can be hard for the union to sort out how to advocate for both of these union members' interests at the same time. Another example: two work units or companies merge, and the union has the difficult task of wrestling with the fairest way to come up with a new seniority list. Should the seniority lists be "dovetailed," or should the "new" employees be placed at the bottom of the existing seniority list? Or, come contract bargaining time, should the big push be to get special pay incentives for senior employees, rewarding them for their length of service, or should it be to raise the salary floor for newly hired folks, who usually are younger and maybe just starting families?

Just as the larger society makes decisions that balance the interests of different groups—whether it's more fair to raise money by raising the income tax rate or the sales tax, for instance—so must our unions.

More Than a Contract

When people think about the role that unions play, the first thing that comes to mind is negotiating over a contract. These collective bargaining agreements deal with what are known as the "terms and conditions of employment." This is unionism at its core: employees banding together to fight for more money, get decent health care and other benefits, and gain more control over many other areas of their day-to-day working lives.

But unions do much more, both directly for those they represent and as a force in society. Union members enjoy a variety of discount programs and other group benefits. If you're like a lot of union members, for example, you purchase your new car through a union discount buying program, you finance that car with a low rate loan through your union credit union, you fill up the gas tank with your union credit card, and you get special union travel discounts when you go on vacation. And you may have researched where to go on that vacation using the AFL-CIO's or another labor-sponsored Internet Service Provider.

My Union, Everyone's Benefits

And there are a lot of other roles that unions play. They may be less visible on a daily basis, but are still extremely significant. For example, many people don't realize that the pay and benefits of workers *without* union representation are shaped in large part by what unions are able to win for their own members. Economists talk about a "union wage effect." This is where the wages of unorganized workers are raised because of the standard established by the unionized workers in a particular locality or industry. There also are laws that require the payment of wages at the "prevailing rate," which almost always means the rate established by the unionized workers in a particular trade. (The best-known of these is the Davis-Bacon law, which applies to federally funded construction projects.)

9

On an even broader scale, the actions of unions in the legislative arena end up protecting all employees, and indeed all Americans. Many laws that benefit everyone would not have been passed without the efforts of organized labor. The establishment of our Social Security system is probably the most important of these. But there are hundreds of other examples of legislation that transformed American society in which organized labor was a key factor, including workplace health and safety and discrimination laws, and unemployment compensation benefits.

Union Movement = Social Justice Movement

In fact, some of organized labor's proudest moments have come at those times in American history where unions took the lead in a fight to improve our society. Martin Luther King, Jr., the Nobel Prize–winning advocate for civil rights for African-Americans and other historically disadvantaged citizens, was gunned down in Memphis in 1968, a day after delivering his "I've Been to the Mountaintop" speech. But how many Americans know that what brought Dr. King to Memphis was the melding of a labor union contract fight and the growing force of the civil rights movement? In a key

IT'S ALL CONNECTED

"Our needs are identical with labor's needs—decent wages, fair working conditions, livable housing, old age security, health and welfare measures, conditions in which families can grow, have education for their children and respect in the community. That is why Negroes support labor's demands and fight laws which curb labor. That is why the labor-hater and labor-baiter is virtually always a twin-headed creature spewing anti-Negro epithets from one mouth and anti-labor propaganda from the other mouth."

—Dr. Martin Luther King, Jr., speaking in support of
striking sanitation workers in Memphis, April 3, 1968

10

moment in both union and civil rights history, African-American sanitation workers organized by the American Federation of State, County and Municipal Employees (AFSCME) were on strike for union recognition and for dignity, united by the slogan "I Am a Man." While strikers were on the picket lines, community supporters pitched in with a boycott of downtown merchants led by the local NAACP and African-American ministers. Dr. King traveled to Memphis because he understood that the union fight to improve wages and benefits was a part of the larger struggle to create a society where Americans of all races would be treated equally.

And there long has been recognition on the union side, as well, that our fight for improved working conditions is connected to the social justice movement in the larger society. One of the few non-African-Americans invited to speak at the 1963 March on Washington for Jobs and Freedom was Walter Reuther, president of the United Auto Workers union (UAW).

Not a Spectator Sport

Unions are far more than a kind of employment insurance policy for working people. True, one face of unions is that they are an organization to which dues must be paid regularly, like insurance premiums are paid to insurance companies, and that these dues buy help in the event that something goes terribly wrong on the job.

But unions are capable of accomplishing a lot more than that. Plenty of union members and union officials have learned the hard way that when workers come to think of their union as a business that provides a service rather than a group of people banding together to fight for common interests, the union quickly loses the clout and credibility needed to defend and advance the members' interests. When an employer looks and sees only a small handful of paid union staff or elected union leaders, and no one standing behind them, pretty soon the employer starts thinking that "the union" isn't really much to contend with. And the truth is, that's right.

HOW YOUR

union operates

You may be in an independent union that represents just a small number of folks in a single workplace. If that's the setup you have, then what you see is what you get: your union is the sum total of you and your co-workers, choosing leaders in your workplace among yourselves, and taking unified action. You have no connections with a national union, like the Machinists or the Teamsters or any of the hundred or so others. And you are not affiliated with the big labor federation, the American Federation of Labor–Congress of Industrial Organizations (AFL-CIO).

Chances are, though, that you are in a union local that is part of a much larger organization with many different levels. Unions come in all shapes and sizes, and just as the political structure of one American city might vary greatly from that of another, different unions govern themselves in different ways.

But there are some basic ways that unions are structured. So let's take a look at how your union is likely to be set up in your particular work unit, and work our way up to—truly—the international level.

The Workplace View

The heart and soul of any union is its members, and they are pulled together by a network of first-line union representatives, often called stewards. Your union may use a different title for this position, such as department rep or representative spokesperson, but the functions will be the same. Stewards are the "eyes and ears" of the union, keeping track for the union of what's happening on a day-to-day basis. An effective steward functions as a two-way pipeline: passing information along to higher-ups in the union, so that they can formulate plans to respond to employer actions, and making sure that the union members in their areas are kept informed about what's going on within the union.

There is no set rule for how many stewards you'll find in a particular workplace, or how many will have responsibility for particular work areas. Sometimes there is a natural organization of the workplace—such as a well-defined work unit, or a particular work shift or one building separated from the rest of a larger facility—so that it makes sense for stewards to be assigned on that basis. So it may be that stewards where you work function according to workplace geography—a steward may be responsible for all union members on a particular floor of a building, for example. Maybe your steward is one who handles matters that directly affect everyone who does your type of job–such as all accountants in a particular government agency, or all nurses aides on a particular wing of a nursing home—or maybe your steward deals with everyone who works on your shift.

Stewards come to be stewards in many different ways. Some unions conduct elections to choose stewards to serve for a specific term of office. In other unions, stewards are appointed, either for a set period of time or indefinitely. Stewards sometimes can spend time during working hours to do their union business, while still getting their regular pay. Some unions provide a stipend for stewards, to compensate them for the extra hours and effort they put in representing members.

Regardless of the formal method for selecting stewards in your workplace, it may well be that most are serving simply because they volunteered. With most unions offering at least some fundamental training in how to do the job of steward, you might want to think about stepping up and playing a more active role in your union in that way.

Union Stewards: First to Be Asked

Your steward is your first point of contact when you have a question about whether your workplace rights have been violated or when you have an idea about some union action that might improve conditions in your workplace. You can't expect a co-worker who has become a union steward to be an

EMPLOYEE INVOLVEMENT PROGRAMS

Most of what unions do, and what most of what this book explains, addresses the essential "us and them" power relationship in the workplace. Without a union, individual employees are at a big disadvantage in trying to protect their interests against a powerful employer. Unions speak collectively for all those in a bargaining unit, negotiating contracts and challenging employer actions through grievances and other means.

But in an increasing number of workplaces, a different structure for labor-management relations has taken hold. These are sometimes in place of the traditional adversary mechanisms and sometimes alongside them. Employee involvement programs, also known by such names as total quality management ("TQM"), quality circles and team concept, are devices by which employees and employer representatives sit side by side (both literally and figuratively) to tackle workplace concerns. In some instances, these have proven to be a valuable means for employees collectively to have significant input into workplace decisions.

But be aware that serious dangers can arise. Some employers establish and manipulate these groups as part of a deliberate strategy of divide and conquer. The idea is that by setting up a forum where the voices of individual employees are heard, the union's role as the collective voice for all its members is weakened. And some union leaders and members discover the hard way that after a period of "cooperation" with the employer, they are unable to challenge a damaging employer initiative because they failed to preserve the union's contract and other rights. Unless clear limits are set on the authority of employee involvement programs, the union and its members can find themselves back in the position of being powerless to affect the important decisions in the workplace.

15

expert on all aspects of workplace rights. But it is a steward's responsibility to do what it takes to find out, if necessary, what action may be appropriate to challenge an employer initiative and to safeguard employees' rights.

Many questions you bring to your steward, or problems you raise, can be dealt with satisfactorily without any type of formal action being taken. It may be that information is the "fix" that's needed, or a conversation between your steward and a management official solves the problem. But sometimes a steward will set in motion a formal action, the most common type being a contract grievance. If the problem or concern that you have calls for a grievance to be filed, then your steward is most likely the "mini-lawyer" who will help draw up and present the grievance and attempt to get it resolved. (What is grievable and what's not, and the procedures used, are covered in some detail in Chapter 7.)

Your steward may take another type of action, as well, to assist you. Your steward is the one with overall responsibility for answering questions about what the employer or the union is doing or could be doing to make things better in the workplace. If the union cannot do something to bring about positive change, your steward should be able to explain why that is.

One Level Up in Your Union

Above the level of steward, the structure of unions varies greatly. But however it is designed, the union in your workplace will be set up in such a way that information is collected, decisions are made, and actions are taken.

It may be, for example, that all of the individual stewards in your workplace report to a chief steward. This person has the responsibility for coordinating all of the grievance activity, including recommending which cases get processed all the way to arbitration—a step taken if the union and the employer can't work out a way to settle a grievance. (See Chapter 8.)

Or your union may have a workplace committee structure, where a grievance committee or a representation committee coordinates all such work. Other union committees may have the responsibility for gathering and passing out information and taking necessary action on a range of other matters, such as health and safety, legislative affairs, or human and civil rights. And sometimes matters such as health and safety are dealt with by joint labor-management committees, consisting of representatives of both the employer and the union.

Sometimes more than one workplace is represented by a single union local (or "chapter," or "lodge" or "branch"; different terms are used by different unions). For example, it may be that the social workers at a number of different hospitals have unionized, and have negotiated contracts for each hospital. But they may all be in a single citywide or statewide union local. Or it may be that a committee structure exists at the level of your local, so that planning and decision making are undertaken at that level. Every local has officers, most likely serving for particular terms that are specified in your union constitution and bylaws, and most likely governed by statutory requirements as to election procedures and other aspects of the union's business.

And at one level or another—in your own local union if it is large enough; or if it's small, then on a regional or national union level—your union will have staff employees doing the full range of union work. Union staff may handle grievance/arbitration advocacy, bargaining, enforcing health and safety standards, or even in-house lawyering. Some union staff are drawn from among the people represented by the union, while others are individuals who have chosen union staff work as their livelihood.

Based on geography or your type of industry or work, your union local is connected in some way with other locals. It may be, for example, that all of the locals of a union in a particular city, county, or even state or larger geographical area unite organizationally to deal with common issues. They can be more effective in addressing concerns they share, or even negotiating jointly, on this broader basis. Or your union may be set up so that different locals representing the same type of employees—such as all county employees, or all of a municipality's blue-collar employees—will be combined organizationally. So your local might be part of a larger structure called a District Council, a Council of Chapters, or something similar.

17

National Connections

You most likely are part of a national union, too. (If your union is called an "international," this means that there are members outside of the fifty states, most often in Canada or Puerto Rico.) The national officers of your union serve for lengths of time determined by the union constitution and bylaws, and sometimes by law. Some unions conduct elections for national officers the same way most other elections are conducted: by secret ballot, usually with each member eligible to cast a vote by mail. Other unions choose to elect their officers at a convention, with delegates usually casting votes based on the number of people they represent. Your national union will also have a fairly sizable governing body, called an Executive Council, Executive Board, or something similar. As with the larger components of the union at other levels, the national union will have paid, full-time staff working with the officers to implement the union's program. At the national level, as well, there is likely to be a committee or departmental structure of some sort, where the work of the union in a particular area (such as legislative work or new organizing) is coordinated.

As a way to combine their resources and increase their effectiveness (and, in part, to respond to mergers and takeovers on the part of employers) in recent years unions have stepped up their pace of mergers and affiliations. In some instances, unions representing workers who perform very similar types of work have decided that it makes more sense to have one bigger union than two smaller unions. One example of this was the merger of the International Ladies Garment Workers Union and the Amalgamated Clothing and Textile Workers Union to form the Union of Needletrades, Industrial and Textile Employees (UNITE). In other instances, union mergers are responses to changes in an industry itself. For example, with new technologies there is increasingly a single information industry, replacing the separate, more distinct enterprises of journalism, the printing trades, and other types of mass communication. To respond to this, a number of smaller unions, including the Newspaper Guild, the Electronic Workers, the Broadcast Technicians, and the International Typographical Union are now all part of the Communications Workers of America.

Unions Work Together

The American Federation of Labor–Congress of Industrial Organizations (AFL-CIO) is an umbrella organization of almost seventy American unions, representing some 13 million workers. Just as businesses band together in chambers of commerce, through the AFL-CIO most American unions at the national level are able to work together on a wide range of common concerns. With officers elected at a convention of AFL-CIO affiliated unions, and a staff based in Washington, D.C., and across the country, the AFL-CIO tries to speak with one voice for the interests of American workers of all types and their unions. Research is done at the national level on areas of concern to working people, analysis of government and social policy is undertaken, ambitious political involvement is coordinated, and efforts are made to mesh the bargaining and organizing agendas of the various affiliated unions. Separate departments seek to zero in on areas of concern to particular types of workers, such as professional employees or those in the building trades. And some projects are undertaken at the national level, such as coordinating the bargaining of all affiliated unions representing workers at a particular company. (While the AFL-CIO includes the vast majority of American labor unions, some, such as the National Education Association, the National Treasury Employees Union and the United Electrical Workers, have chosen to remain independent, outside the AFL-CIO structure.)

Below the national level, too, your union probably has connections with other unions or with other organizations with compatible goals. It's often the case that more than one union will represent different types of employees of a single employer (or even in a single facility). In such cases, the different locals often realize that they will have more power if they work cooperatively. This can take a number of different forms. For example, there may be regular meetings of the different locals, simply to share information about what the employer is up to and what locals are doing to protect their members' interests. Some locals band together to take effective joint action, such as coordinating their bargaining, so that the employer cannot easily play off one group against the others.

And on a geographical basis, as well, unions often have ongoing organizational relationships. For example, the AFL-CIO has state federations and central labor councils, which are networks of the different unions that represent employees in a particular city or county or larger geographical area. These councils are used to work for common purpose on legislative matters (such as endorsing or campaigning for a particular candidate, or fighting for or against proposed legislation), or for supporting one another in organizing drives or in battles with a local employer.

19

International Connections

Increasingly, companies operate in many different countries, and each country's national trade policy is determined by what goes on everywhere in the world. Nearly every day we can read in the newspaper about a U.S. company pulling up stakes and moving some or all of its operation to another country (or blackmailing workers and communities by threatening to do so) or coming up with new production methods that transform the products

AN EXAMPLE OF INTERNATIONAL UNION SOLIDARITY: THE UPS STRIKE

The strike in the summer of 1997 against United Parcel Service was a landmark event for American labor. The Teamsters' fight against UPS's increasing use (make that "abuse") of part-timers and its expansion of subcontracting struck a responsive chord in millions of Americans. The final strike settlement forced the company to cut back significantly in its exploitation of part-time workers by creating new full-time jobs, providing for wage increases for part-timers and placing contractual limits on subcontracting.

Many factors contributed to the victory. The UPS workers—both full-timers and part-timers—stood firm in their strike, and other unionized workers and the American public generally lent strong support. But all the world was a stage for this labor struggle. Just as UPS is a worldwide company (operating in over 200 countries, with 185,000 workers in the United States, and 340,000 employees globally) unionists around the world worked in solidarity on the labor side of the equation.

Under the umbrella of one of the International Trade Secretariats (the International Transport Workers Federation), the Teamsters developed a truly international strategy. Well in advance of the actual strike, this international group set up an information-sharing network and support structure. When the strike call went out, workers at key UPS air hubs and distribution centers worldwide held demonstrations and went out on sympathy strikes in support of their American union brothers and sisters.

While most of the support action took place in Western Europe, the workers' effort was truly global. In the Philippines, for example, a union-organized motorcade of 100 cars surrounded a UPS subcontractor, shutting down the movement of packages for an entire day. And in India, where UPS relies largely on railroads to move its goods, the railroad workers' union refused to handle UPS packages during the strike.

they make into truly international products. Fierce political fights have broken out over what kind of restrictions should be placed on international trade and the mobility of international capital and labor, including such disputes as the one over adoption of the North American Free Trade Agreement (NAFTA), and the one over trade with China, where workers are paid much less than their American counterparts and are not allowed to unionize.

And so unions combine their efforts across national borders. In order to respond effectively to these challenges, American unions participate in the International Confederation of Free Trade Unions (ICFTU), an international trade union organization representing more than 123 million workers from 145 countires, and more than a dozen International Trade Secretariats, consisting of unionists from every continent who work in related industries. For example, the American labor unions representing those in the food and beverage industry are part of a group called the International Union of Food, Agricultural, Hotel, Restaurant, Catering, Tobacco and Allied Workers' Associations (IUF), to which 326 organizations from 118 countries belong. To advance their efforts on behalf of the 10 million workers they represent, through the IUF these unions can exchange information and try to come up with common positions and actions that will benefit their members worldwide. (Organizations participating in International Trade Secretariats also include some not affiliated with the AFL-CIO. Education International, for example, includes the National Education Association, with more than 2 million members, as well as the American Association of University Professors, a national advocacy organization speaking exclusively for college and university educators.)

Another international organization deserves mention, as well. The first president of the AFL, Samuel Gompers, worked hard in the aftermath of World War I to establish the International Labor Organization (ILO). This organization, now a specialized international agency of the United Nations, has a tripartite structure, meaning equal representation from governments, employers, and worker organizations. It seeks to open up a "social dialog" to deal with international problems directly affecting workers and to elevate the standards for workers around the world.

21

A

member's rights

AND RESPONSIBILITIES

Since you're working in a unionized workplace, because of its role as "exclusive representative" your union is entitled—in fact, required by law–to represent every individual in the bargaining unit. But just the same, the law says that you cannot be forced to become a full, dues-paying member. Depending on a variety of factors—the state you work in, whether you are a public sector or private sector employee, and what your union contract provides—it may be that the most you can be required to pay is a portion of the full dues. You may even be able to get away with paying nothing at all. If that sounds tempting, you might want to think about other ways you could save a few bucks: not spending money to replace bald tires (a good idea until you hit a slippery stretch of road), or holding off on fixing your leaky roof (no problem, unless it should happen to rain), or not getting your children inoculated against polio.

Practical Aspects of Membership

Before going into an explanation of the different categories of what is called "union security," let's take a look at why becoming a full union member is the right thing to do.

You Get to Participate in Decision Making

Paying union dues is your ticket to having a say in what the union does. Just as when we get fed up with the voting record of one of our elected legislators, and we "vote the bum out" in the next election, union members have the same system of checks and balances for union officers. If you're dissatisfied with the quality of union leadership, the solution is to support other candidates in the next elections. But you've got the vote only if you're a member.

And around contract bargaining time, only dues-paying members of the union are eligible to participate in making many critical decisions. For example, many unions conduct a prebargaining poll—but only of members—to determine priorities at the bargaining table. And virtually all unions permit only full dues-paying members to vote on whether or not to ratify the final contract agreement. No membership, no say in the process. No membership, no right to vote on the outcome.

You Send a Message

Union officials and staff members keep a very close watch on the number of represented employees who join the union and pay dues. They understand that having the resources to do their jobs well depends in large part on the union having enough money. But savvy union leaders also understand that someone else is keenly interested in how many choose to join and how many try to freeload: the boss. Those on the other side understand full well that the more limited the union's resources, the less effective it will be. A strong, voluntary union membership also gets the message across to the employer that the individual employees are standing behind their leaders, so that when a union official addresses the employer, it's understood that one voice speaks for many.

Everything Costs Something

The ultimate strength of the union lies in the determination and participation of its members. But it's also true that it takes money for an organization to translate good intentions into concrete actions. What use is negotiating a collective bargaining agreement with strong protections if the union doesn't afterwards have the money needed to process grievances to arbitration when the employer chooses to ignore what the contract says? How effective can your union be if there is no money to pay rent for office space or a phone, to hire knowledgeable staff to answer your questions on the phone, or to bring in health and safety experts to advise on hazards in the workplace? Everyone needs to pitch in financially to make the union strong.

Information Is Power

Your union probably provides more comprehensive information to dues-paying members than to other represented employees. Some of this is based on fairness: those who are footing the bill for the organization's work deserve more detailed information on what the organization is doing. But some of this is also an outgrowth of the union having to choose which activities it can realistically engage in with the limited resources available: with not everyone paying dues, it may just be too expensive to send the union newsletter to non-members, for example. So if you want to be in the loop as to the labor-management relations activity that affects every minute of your workplace life, that's another good reason to pony up your union dues.

Plus, It's the Fair Thing

Think about the relationship between a government and its citizens. Each of us approves of many of the decisions made on our behalf by our elected representatives but disapproves of others. Imagine the foolishness of trying to have a society where each person decided things based only on what was best for him or her individually. The fact is, we all benefit from understanding that the only practical way to live together is to have a group of people with common interests making group decisions. So each of us pays taxes, with the understanding that our pooled funds generally are used for the common good. In most cases, it's simply not practical to allow individuals to "opt out" of society's decisions. You, for example, may not have school-age children, but it would hardly be realistic for you to pay a slightly lower percentage of taxes because you don't directly benefit from (or even approve of) spending on public education. (One of this country's most distinguished Supreme Court justices, Oliver Wendell Holmes, put it succinctly: "Taxes are the price of civilization.") Or you may have a neighbor who doesn't think that the stop sign on the corner is really necessary, but you sure want her to obey it if your kid is trying to cross the street.

The relationship between a union and those it represents is the same as between a nation and its citizens. Unions exist because employees see that dealing with an employer only as individuals ultimately puts each of us in a weaker position. So we make the decision to work together as a group, and to have our elected union representatives implement decisions on behalf of the group. Will you agree with every single decision made by your union? Not a chance. But just the same, you and every other represented employee in your workplace benefits overall from the group decisions and actions.

You may have thought in the last round of bargaining, for example, that the union should have pushed harder to improve the health benefits package. But the negotiated increase in wages that was won instead translated into more money in your paycheck.

So, just as with taxes, fairness dictates that everyone pays their rightful share of union dues. Everyone benefits from many of the uses to which our dues money is put, and is not pleased with some other uses. That's the nature of being a part of any group, be it a community association, a sports league, or a labor union.

The Law and Union Membership

What are your obligations of union membership and payment of dues? Much depends on the state in which you are employed and whether your employer is covered by the National Labor Relations Act or by a public sector bargaining statute or other law. But here's a rundown of some of the basic principles.

Union Shop/Agency Shop

These terms refer to workplaces where new employees are required within a certain period of time to begin paying toward what's needed for the union to do its work. A "union security" provision in your contract may state that you are required to become a member of the union within thirty or sixty days of being hired, as a condition of keeping your job. What is being required in these cases is not full, dues-paying membership in the union but rather the regular payment of a defined amount of money, which can be somewhat less than full dues. (There's another type of arrangement, known as "maintenance of membership," in which all those who are members of the union as of a certain date are required to maintain their memberships for a set period of time.) In the private sector, all these kinds of arrangements are bargained in the union contract. In the public sector, they may come about through bargaining or legislation.

If you are covered by this kind of union security arrangement, the law says you can choose not to pay the full amount. You may opt, instead, to pay what is called an "agency fee" or "fair share." You must pay one or the other, however; if you do not join the union or pay your fair share, you can lose your job.

LEGITIMATE AND NOT-SO-LEGITIMATE OBJECTIONS TO UNION MEMBERSHIP

Since shouldering the full cost of the work done on behalf of you and others by your union is the right thing to do, in most instances there is no justification for refusing to join the union.

But there is a category recognized by law that can be distinguished in a fundamental way from those individuals who don't appreciate the collective nature of union representation, or who simply are too cheap to pay full freight. Special provisions in the National Labor Relations Act, as well as in public sector bargaining laws, permit employees whose religious beliefs preclude full union membership to opt out of what would otherwise be their financial obligations. This often takes the form of allowing them instead to make payments equivalent to union dues and fees to a designated charity.

Most objections to full union dues don't arise out of such decisions of conscience, however. A tremendous amount of costly and time-consuming litigation that has diverted substantial union resources from the job of representing members has been sponsored by anti-union outfits such as the National Right to Work Committee, a group supported—no surprise here—by employers. The huge drain on union resources caused by this litigation (with cases going all way up to the United States Supreme Court) yields just what employers want: unions that are weak because they lack the financial resources to fight on behalf of their members. So it's not hard to see why many in the union movement refer to the group sponsoring much of this litigation as the "National Right to Work *For Less* Committee."

27

You may opt to pay only a reduced agency fee, as determined by the well-known 1988 *Beck* decision of the Supreme Court and by many other cases. Your union usually is required to set the amount of that fee based on a calculation of what percentage of dues money is used for collective bargaining purposes. These "chargeable" expenses are those arising out of your union's representation activities: the costs of bargaining a contract, processing grievances and taking cases to arbitration, training union representatives, and other day-to-day expenses faced by the union in the course of promoting the interests of members of the bargaining unit. Unfortunately, a series of court decisions has taken a pretty narrow view of what makes up the union's "nonchargeable" expenses, that is, ones that nonmembers are not required to contribute to. Items such as political contributions, lobbying expenses, and social activities open only to union members cannot be included in the agency fee calculation. Despite the fact that these activities all help build union strength—and benefit everyone represented by the union—nonmembers can be given the legal "right" to decline to pay their fair share.

Still, agency fee payers have a broad range of legal rights. Unions in the private sector are required by the National Labor Relations Act to notify nonmembers annually of the calculation of the amount of agency fee required, to disclose financial information verified by an independent audit to back up that calculation, and to allow objecting nonmembers to pursue challenges before an impartial decision maker prior to any amount in question being spent by the union.

Open Shop

Because of actions taken by state legislatures, twenty-one states—in the South, Midwest and Southwest—are "right to work" states. This commonly used term is actually quite misleading since the "right" given by these laws is not in any sense the right to be employed. Rather, those working in a "right to work" state have the "right" to enjoy some of the benefits of union protection without paying a cent for them. For private sector employees in such states, as well as for a number of public sector workers across the country, as a matter of law individuals may not be required to contribute financially to the cost of that representation. Workplaces covered by this type of arrangement are referred to as "open shops." Dues-paying members often refer to workers who refuse to pay their fair share for the union's work as "freeloaders" or "leeches."

Closed Shop

The term "closed shop" refers to a workplace where you won't be hired unless you're already a member of the union. Such arrangements are illegal, although they shouldn't be confused with union "hiring halls," where the union can serve as an exclusive source of referrals for job openings, a standard practice in the construction industry.

Dues: The Nuts and Bolts

There is tremendous variation from one union to another as to how dues amounts are set. And it is quite possible that the different components of your union dues (local, district or other intermediate body, and national/international) are calculated using different formulas and changed in different ways. The formula used for determining what your union dues are, and the mechanisms that are in place for making any changes, usually are found in the constitution and bylaws of the union at the various levels.

How Dues Amounts Are Determined

Sometimes dues are set at a flat dollar amount. If your union uses this approach, then you and all of your co-workers pay the identical amount in dues, regardless of the fact that your earnings may vary by quite a bit. This system has the advantages of simplicity and predictability of income flow for the union. But some unions opt for a "progressive" dues structure, preferring a system where those who earn more pay more.

Rather than setting dues at a dollar amount, some unions establish dues as a percentage of salary. When this method is used, everyone in the bargaining unit pays dues based on the same percentage. This has the effect of "socializing" the cost, since those who earn more pay more under such a formula.

Or your union may use a variation, with the amount of union dues determined by brackets of earnings. Under such a setup, everyone who makes within a certain range pays a certain number of dollars in dues, everyone who makes somewhat more money pays a higher dollar amount in dues, and so on.

Dues Increases

Your union dues may be set at a particular dollar amount, with any increases determined by whatever democratic procedures are in place for such decision making. The required processes sometimes are specified by law or by your union's constitution, and may include requiring a membership meeting where a secret ballot vote is taken, or holding a membership referendum. Sometimes it can be done by action of elected convention delegates. Or a mechanism may be in place from the outset that automatically provides for annual or other periodic increases. For example, your union may have voted to establish a dollar amount for dues that is pegged to an hourly rate or a salary set by your collective bargaining agreement. So when an annual contractual raise kicks in, this automatically adjusts the dollar amount of the dues upward, as well.

29

If your dues are set by formula as a percentage of your earnings, then this automatically results in an increase in your dues obligation as your earnings rise over time.

Initiation Fees and Assessments

Many unions require an initiation fee to be paid when you first join. Sometimes the amount is quite modest. In some industries, such as the building trades, it is not unusual to have initiation fees amount to a lot of money. This practice recognizes that new workers generally are starting their jobs at pay and benefit levels achieved only after years of struggle by current (and even long-retired) members of the union, levels unlikely to be found at a non-union employer. The one-time fees are generally viewed by the union as a reasonable "entry fee" to compensate the union for the work it performed that allow a new hire to start off at fair pay and benefit rates, with even higher pay and benefits assured via the collective bargaining agreement currently in place. Most unions have a system in place for obtaining an "honorable withdrawal" card if you do leave your union job for a period of time, so that you don't have to pay a new initiation fee if you come back to work in a unionized shop.

In addition to regular dues, your union local or national union may have an assessment of one sort or another, such as to fund strike benefits or new organizing projects.

The Mechanics of Paying Dues

In the early days of unions, the method by which workers paid their union dues was wonderfully straightforward and uncomplicated. On payday, the shop steward would come around and collect from each worker the nickel or dime that constituted union dues. This simple procedure clearly had advantages: like it or not, it compelled each union representative to have one-on-one contact with each union member on a regular basis. But the drawbacks are easy to identify: especially in large workplaces, this was a tremendously time-consuming and cumbersome process for all concerned, stewards and members alike.

These days, there are much easier—though more impersonal—ways that unions collect dues. Most workplaces have the option of a checkoff from your pay. Just as taxes, savings and other regular payments are automatically deducted from your paycheck, so too are union dues. Just as you have to fill out a form when you start your job to trigger your payroll deduction of taxes, automatic payroll deduction of union dues requires you to sign on the dotted line as well.

Some employees pay their union dues in other ways. You may, for example, simply write a check, either every payday, monthly, or even annually. Or, you may be able to authorize automatic payment from your bank checking or savings account or your credit union.

Be aware that the amount of your union dues may qualify as a tax deduction. As they say, consult your tax adviser. . . .

THE UNION'S

responsibility

TO ITS MEMBERS

We've discussed the union's right to speak collectively for all in the bargaining unit—the concept of exclusive representation. Now let's take a look at the other side of the coin: the union's obligation to represent the interests of each individual in the unit. This requirement, that the union advocate for all in a bargaining unit, not just some, is called the duty of fair representation, or DFR.

The Duty of Fair Representation

There are no hard and fast rules for what the union must do to live up to its duty of fair representation. There isn't even a precise definition of what that obligation consists of. When the United States Supreme Court and the National Labor Relations Board have wrestled with the meaning and extent of this obligation over the years, they have described it in such ways as "an honest effort to serve the interest of all . . . without hostility to any" and the right of bargaining unit members to be free from "unfair or irrelevant or insidious treatment" by their union representatives. The catch phrase often used is that unions breach their obligation when they engage in actions that are "arbitrary, discriminatory or in bad faith."

For example, a union steward cannot refuse to help a worker with a grievance just because he personally dislikes the worker.

But the union obligation to represent the interests of all unit members fairly does not translate into a legal obligation always to speak for each individual member, or to be flawless in performing its representation duties. Let's take a look at each of these.

Balancing Different Interests

When a given issue arises, different individuals or groups within the bargaining unit may well have different and conflicting stakes in possible outcomes. For example, in contract negotiations the union can push for raises calculated as a percentage of salary or for raises as a flat dollar amount. The first formula puts more money in the pockets of those who already earn more, while the second ends up providing a greater percentage salary increase to lower-paid employees. There may be lots of good policy arguments for and against each of these alternatives, but in the end, whatever decision is made is going to be better financially for one group and worse for the other. Since there's no way around this, the union is obligated only to act fairly in how it decides which direction to go, not to somehow come up with a magical solution that is perfect for everyone.

Perfection *Not* Required

Nor is the union held to an impossible standard of being flawless in the performance of its duties. Suppose, for example, that your workplace is flooded by grievances and that your steward misplaces some paperwork and fails to process your grievance in a timely fashion. As regrettable as such an oversight is, some legal cases have found that this is just "mere negligence" and is not enough to violate the union's duty of fair representation. But don't think that the union has a free ride to decide it won't carry out its responsibilities capably and fairly. For example, if the reason that your grievance was not processed in a timely way by the union was because of some personal grudge against you, you certainly would have a strong legal claim that the union therefore violated its DFR. Or if a particular steward or your local union in general has a pattern of failing to process grievances competently, that as well would add up to a strong claim of a breach of the duty of fair representation.

The two examples given above are by far the most common situations in which allegations arise that the union has breached its DFR. With respect to the grievance/arbitration procedure, you may feel that a grievance you wish to pursue is not handled properly, or you may take issue with the union's decision not to take a particular grievance all the way to arbitration. Or you may believe the union acted improperly by not deciding even to initiate a grievance on your behalf. For example, the union may not feel that your case is winnable, because the contract language does not support your claim, or because it will be unable to prove the necessary facts to win the case. So long as the union investigated any conflicting claims before it made a good faith decision not to pursue the grievance, it has acted lawfully.

On the contract bargaining front, arriving at an agreement with the employer ultimately depends on reaching a series of mutually acceptable compromises. So the bargaining process, by its nature, results in individual bargaining unit members having different degrees of satisfaction with the final agreement. And even coming up with the union's initial bargaining proposals necessarily involves weighing and balancing the sometimes competing interests of different groups within the union membership.

There are other situations, as well, in which the union's duty of fair representation may be an issue. If you exercise your right to have a union representative present when you're being questioned by the employer (discussed in Chapter 10) you have the right to expect a certain level of competence on the part of the representative your union provides. Or if you consult the union about a health and safety concern, or about another aspect of workplace rights, you similarly are entitled to a reasonable effort on the part of the union to give you guidance.

If Your Rights May Have Been Violated

If you believe that your union has not lived up to its duty of fair representation, or even if you have concerns about the quality of the representation provided, your first step is to sort out what happened and why. It's simply not fair to your co-workers who have stepped forward to do the union's work to react by making accusations without first checking out the facts. So approach your steward, or anyone else who had responsibility for the action you are unhappy about, state your concerns, and try to listen with an open mind to whatever explanations are offered. Just as with dealing with an employer representative, you may want to be cautious and have a third party present for such a discussion.

Evaluate the explanation that is offered. Try to be objective. You may not like the fact that the union didn't "take your side," but try to take a step back and see whether the decision that was made might have been a reasonable and fair one under the circumstances, one attempting to balance the different needs and interests of different individuals.

If you are not satisfied with the explanation that you have been given, you may have a number of options. There may be an internal union procedure, set up so that union members can air complaints about actions the union has taken. Some unions have quite elaborate mechanisms, including neutral, outside parties who come in and review the circumstances. Alternatively, there may be formal legal action you can take, including filing an unfair labor practice charge or a lawsuit alleging a violation of the duty of fair representation. You may well need to consult with an attorney, or with a worker advocacy group, to sort out what your legal rights are.

Dig Deeper for Solutions?

But before choosing to assert any individual legal rights you may have regarding your union, give some thought to analyzing the underlying problem. If you were the unfortunate victim of a single incompetent steward, this may not be the union's "fault" in any real sense. To be fair to the union as a whole, you might want to decline to press any legal claim you might have. On the other hand, the treatment by the union that you are unhappy about may be part of a much larger problem that the union has. It may be that the top leadership is not fairly taking into account the legitimate interests of large groups of members, or falls so short in its leadership ability that the entire organization has become weak and ineffective. If this is the case, the solution to the problem is larger than whatever you might hope to achieve in pursuing an individual duty of fair representation legal claim. What is needed is a change in the elected leadership, or at least for those individuals to receive a wake-up call. If this is the situation that your local is in, then you and your or co-workers should give some thought to how to exercise your democratic rights as union members to change the direction of the union. (Information on those rights is found in the next section, Internal Union Rights.)

Alternative Relief?

Finally, don't lose sight of the fact that you may have the ability to pursue independently whatever your underlying complaint was, even if the union hasn't acted on your behalf. For example, if the union elected not to pursue a grievance in which you alleged unlawful discrimination, you may well have the right to go to a state or federal agency, or to court, to pursue your discrimination claim on your own. (But since the union will not be involved, you will need to weigh any financial costs associated with pursuing such a legal action unassisted.)

Internal Union Rights

As individual Americans we have a host of legal rights that attempt to guarantee our participation in a democratic society: free speech rights; the right to obtain information about what our elected leaders and government do in our name; and the right to vote. Let's take a look at the rights that you have, as a union member, to participate in the democratic workings of your collective bargaining representative.

The primary law setting forth your legal rights to participate in your union grows out of a federal statute passed in 1959, known as the Landrum-Griffin Act. Specifically, the Labor Management Reporting and Disclosure Act (LMRDA), administered by the U.S. Department of Labor, covers unions with members in the private sector. (If your union represents both public and private sector workers, this law may apply to you, as it will if you are a postal service employee.) While this discussion will center on the LMRDA, the concepts and rights contained in that statute are generally similar to those that apply to public sector union members, as well.

37

Speaking Up, at Union Meetings and Elsewhere

As a union member, you enjoy a broad set of rights similar in many ways to the rights found in the First Amendment to the U.S. Constitution. The LMRDA's "Bill of Rights of Members of Labor Organizations" contains an "equal rights" provision, guaranteeing all union members the right to nominate candidates for union office, to vote in union elections, and to attend and participate in union meetings. While the federal law does not require labor organizations to hold meetings, it does say that when meetings are held you have the right to participate fully. (Keep in mind that there's another source of rights you may have related to holding union meetings, electing officers, and voting on dues increases in new contract agreements: your union's constitution and bylaws. So even though the law may not require your union to hold a meeting, your local's constitution and bylaws probably will contain such a provision.)

The labor "Bill of Rights" also guarantees "freedom of speech and assembly." The law does say that unions are allowed to have "reasonable rules" regarding how it runs its affairs. But you, the union member, have a guaranteed right to have and to express your viewpoints on the union and those who lead and participate in it, even if those viewpoints are critical or negative ones.

Union Elections

While the decision whether to hold meetings may be left to the discretion of a union, a different rule applies as to holding elections for union officers and conducting a referendum on dues increases or other financial assessments of members. At least for unions covered by the LMRDA, there are detailed requirements dealing with the frequency of elections for union officers at all the various levels of a union, and how those elections must be conducted (including requirements as to types of balloting—on the jobsite, by mail, and so forth). At the local level, your union must provide for election of officers by secret ballot, and it must do so no less frequently than every three years.

Union Financial Information

Whether under the LMRDA or similar public sector laws, unions generally are required to file various information reports with a government agency and to make the information available to their members. For private sector employees, these Labor Management or "LM" reports are public information, available to you from the local office of the federal Department of Labor, or by ordering from that agency's website (www.dol.gov). They are worth tracking down if you wish to obtain detailed information as to a union's financial status, such as assets and liabilities, salaries and expenses of union officers and staff, and any loans the union may have granted to members or businesses.

Protection and Enforcement

The LMRDA also protects your exercise of internal union rights by making it illegal for a union to "fine, suspend, expel, or otherwise discipline any of its members for exercising any right to which he is entitled." So a union can't discipline a member for expressing unpopular viewpoints, for forming an opposition caucus within the union, or for campaigning for candidates who oppose incumbent union officers.

In fact, cases have held that in the rough and tumble of union politics, unions cannot discipline members who make untrue statements about union officers. But keep in mind that there are limits, of course, to these rights you have within your union: the law will not, for example, protect you if you publicly call upon your co-workers to quit the union and join a rival union. If the union does have justification for initiating a disciplinary action against you, it must provide certain due process protections (such as written notice of the specific charges against you and a fair opportunity to respond to them) and it must follow the procedures that are in its own constitution and bylaws.

The LMRDA is enforced by the Department of Labor and the courts.

Trusteeships

Most unions at the national or state level have the authority under certain circumstances to impose what are known as trusteeships (sometimes known as "receiverships") on locals. During the imposition of trusteeship, a union local loses control over its assets and the day-to-day running of union affairs. For as long as the trusteeship is in force, an individual appointed by the national union assumes this day-to-day authority. Periodic reports must be filed detailing the reason the trusteeship was imposed and reporting on all of the financial implications.

The law says that a union may be placed into trusteeship only for certain reasons, and whatever procedures are outlined in the union's constitution and bylaws must be followed. Trusteeships often serve useful purposes in weeding out pockets of corruption in union locals, and in helping locals that are in trouble because of extreme fiscal mismanagement or political infighting get back on their feet. At the same time, there have been abuses of the authority to impose trusteeships, where a national union has tried simply to impose its will on a local.

In the very unlikely event that your local is placed into trusteeship, and you do not think that this action is in the best interest of the members, you have the right as an individual member to initiate a challenge. A complaint on your part can trigger an inquiry into whether proper grounds exist for placing your local in trusteeship and whether the necessary procedures were followed.

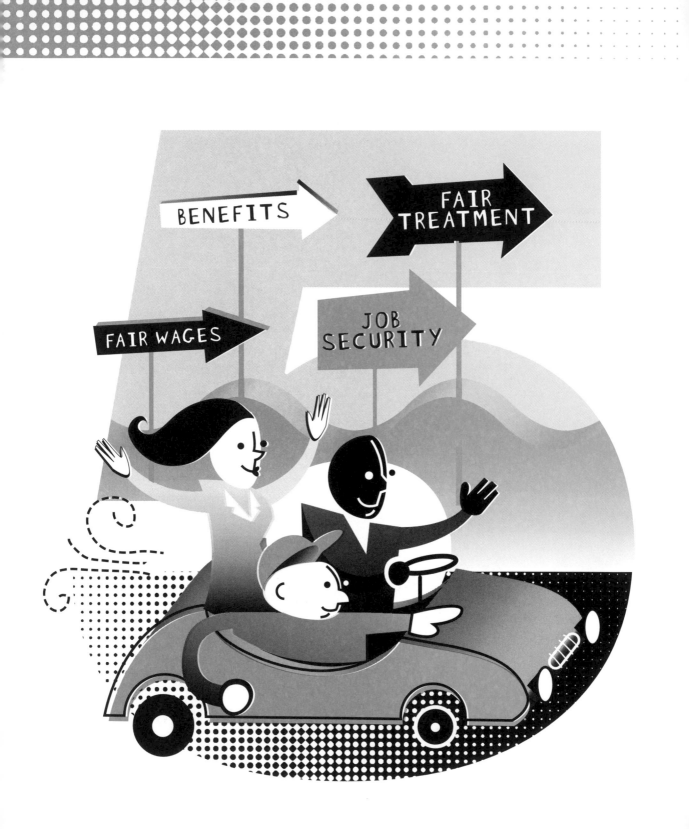

YOUR

union contract:

GETTING THERE

Society functions under a set of laws passed by legislators. The workplace functions under a collective bargaining agreement negotiated by the union and the employer. Both serve the same purpose: creating a set of binding rules on what is permitted and what is prohibited.

How does a contract get negotiated? Sometimes the law under which a particular union and employer operate sets out specific procedures for reaching a collective bargaining agreement. Or in the union contract itself, your union and employer may have agreed upon a set of rules for how the next contract is to be negotiated. Exactly how the bargaining process shapes up will be determined in large part by whether you are in the public or private sector, and by the ground rules or history of the parties in your industry or workplace. For example, in some industries—such as auto manufacturing or the U.S. Postal Service—a national contract is bargained, and sometimes only certain issues are then subject to negotiations at the local level. In others—at newspapers, for example, or your local police or fire department—every issue is worked out right there.

But a lot of the general process of getting a new contract looks pretty much the same, no matter what type of work you do, who employs you, or what union represents you.

The Bargaining Process

The formal bargaining process generally begins when the union presents its proposals at the negotiating table, at a time and place agreed to by both sides. Either at that session or later on, the employer usually brings in proposals of its own.

How does a union come up with what its bargaining agenda will be? The process the union goes through to figure out what proposals to present usually includes looking at:

♦ what the workforce's experience has shown is "broken" in the old contract, and what therefore needs to get "fixed" in the new one;

♦ how to balance the needs and expectations of various groups of employees represented by the union (for example, professional and clerical employees in the same bargaining unit, or day shift and night shift workers, or newer employees and those with greater seniority), which will sometimes be quite different or even in conflict;

♦ what the union itself needs so it can function as an effective advocate for its members (like getting time off for union stewards so they can process grievances);

♦ the reality of what's happening in other workplaces, or in society generally. (Is inflation so high that it's reasonable to expect substantial raises? Are health care costs increasing so fast that everyone is either paying more or seeing benefits get trimmed? Is your employer facing hard times or is it flush with cash?)

Surveying the Members

Unions begin preparations for bargaining by educating their members about how and when bargaining will take place, and what the issues may be. To find out what's on your mind, your union may hold meetings to ask you and your co-workers directly what problems you'd like your negotiators to tackle in bargaining. Very often some sort of written survey is distributed to determine what the top priorities should be, and how important each one is in the members' eyes. (This communication is a two-way street: savvy union negotiators use questionnaires or newsletters early on not only to gather information but also to educate members on the issues that probably will be major areas of labor-management conflict in bargaining. Used this way, a bargaining survey is a tool to begin to build unity.)

Whether it's a written questionnaire or a workplace meeting, this first stage is your opportunity to weigh in on the things in your working life that you'd like to see changed through bargaining. At the beginning and then throughout the bargaining process, if your steward, bargaining committee members and other union leaders don't know what you and your co-workers really want, how can you get it?

Selecting the Bargaining Team

There's no "one size fits all" for bargaining committees, since the size and makeup of each workplace is different. Bargaining a contract requires a tremendous amount of time and effort, in both face-to-face negotiations and in each side doing separate preparation and research. Teams need to be small enough to get the work done efficiently. But it also makes sense for a union bargaining team to be large enough to include people with a close understanding of the needs of the various types of people in the bargaining unit. Whether the differences are those of day and night workers, skilled and unskilled, male and female, different races or cultural groups, or anything else, the union needs some way of making sure that the bargaining team can speak forcefully and accurately for all members.

By the way, don't assume that just because you've never bargained a contract before, it's out of the question that you could be included on the bargaining team. It can be a smart move for unions to put a couple of less experienced people on the bargaining committee, as a way of grooming the next generation of negotiators. And newer members on a negotiating team can bring a fresh perspective that is helpful to the more experienced hands.

There are other ways, too, that you can be involved in the bargaining process. Think about asking to work on a union bargaining subcommittee that will have the job of researching the issues or digging up facts to respond to what the employer's pushing for. Or, if your union does this, you could volunteer to be a special bargaining representative for your work area. Your job then is to help the union negotiators by distributing information on what's happening at the table—through handing out flyers or holding small worksite meetings—and to function as the union's "eyes and ears" on the shop floor, so that the union bargaining team can keep alert to what the members are thinking. Or you may be able to serve on a special bargaining council, usually a pretty large group set up so that representatives from each work area can advise the bargaining team throughout negotiations.

Face-to-Face Negotiations

The bargaining process always includes face-to-face sessions, conducted in a fairly formal way. Notes are taken, for example, so the parties will have a record of what was said if a dispute later comes up over what did or didn't happen during the talks. Depending on the type of union and the type and size of the bargaining unit, negotiations for the union will be done either by a single spokesman or by individual bargaining teams, with each addressing a specific area of concern. The bargainers present proposals and the facts, figures and arguments that justify them. Since the other side has proposals of its own, the sessions also include asking questions about what they're proposing and why, and debating the facts and arguments.

Bargaining is a process of give and take (with each side, of course, trying to take as much as it can and give as little as possible). Throughout negotiations, each party meets in between sessions and holds caucuses—that is, meetings of its members only—during the middle of bargaining sessions. This time is used by each side to sort through which of its proposals it needs to keep pushing for, and which of the other side's it may be willing to agree to. Issue by issue, the parties explore areas of compromise to see where agreement can be reached.

As the bargaining process goes on, the union may report back to the membership what items the parties have agreed to, and where the conflicts are. Sometimes members will be allowed—or even encouraged by the union—to sit in on bargaining sessions. If you can, take the opportunity to see firsthand how the union presents the employees' point of view, and how the employer responds to the union's agenda. It can be a real eye opener to witness the employer's representatives "just say no" to things you know are totally reasonable. And it sends a useful message to the other side, too, when they see union members willing to take the time to show up and visibly support their bargaining team.

Bargaining a contract from start to finish can take quite a bit of time, with agreements being reached point by point until the entire new contract is in place. Sometimes, bargaining is not wrapped up by the time the old contract has expired. When that happens, one of two things takes place:

either the parties keep bargaining or there is a showdown then and there. Depending on a number of legal factors and what the parties work out, if bargaining continues past the expiration date of the old contract, sometimes the terms of the old contract will remain in effect, anyway. So even though in some ways you're in between contracts, your employer still has to do what the old contract required.

Concluding an Agreement

Even when the parties reach agreement at the table on all items, it's usually not yet a done deal. Others often must approve these "tentative agreements" before they are signed, sealed and delivered. On the employer side, sometimes a board of directors or higher-ups in the organization will have to give their approval, or the legislature will have to fund a public sector contract wage or benefit increase. On the union side, either the union bylaws or the practice of the union usually provides for member ratification of the agreement—a vote to accept or reject. (Keep in mind, though, that there are some situations when you won't get to vote approval or disapproval of a contract; for example, if a settlement ultimately is handed down by an outside arbitrator, as described later.)

Either at a union meeting or through printed material or a union website, you should be provided a full opportunity to educate yourself on the provisions of the tentative agreement. Usually, the bargaining team or the union leadership will make a recommendation on whether the contract should be voted up or down. Your union leaders may well recommend a "no" vote on the contract, as a tactic. A vote by the rank and file to send the union negotiators back to the bargaining table is sometimes an effective way of showing the employer's negotiators that what's been offered just isn't enough to settle the contract.

Actual voting on a contract can take place through a mail ballot or at a union meeting where the vote may be by either open or secret ballot. Almost always, only dues-paying members of the union get to vote on accepting or rejecting the contract. And just as in elections for U.S. president or for legislative representatives, the outcome is determined by those who take the time and trouble to vote; when you choose not to cast a vote in the democratic process of contract ratification, you are letting others decide for you what law of the workplace you will live under.

When you are faced with the often difficult decision of whether to ratify a tentative agreement on a new contract, keep in mind that this vote is

45

IT'S NOT JUST THE "UNION CONTRACT"

Don't be misled by the term "union contract." Understandably, people call it that because the union negotiates it. But every contract is a deal struck by two parties and is binding on both. In the case of a collective bargaining agreement, this means that your employer and your union have gone through a process of give and take. At the end they reached an agreement under which employees and the employer have both rights and obligations. So it's not really just the "union contract," it's the "union and employer" contract, and both sides have to live by it.

Understand, too, that a union contract is fundamentally different from other contracts you're used to, say a contract to buy a house or a used car. In such private contracts, we're unlikely to accept terms we don't like; if the price the dealer asks for the car is too high, we simply don't sign a contract to buy it at that price, and we look around for a better deal. But a collective bargaining agreement reflects the relative power between the union and the employer. You and your union may not be pleased with some of the terms in a contract settlement, but you may not have the wherewithal to reject a deal on those terms. A bad contract provision can't simply be sent back to the kitchen like an undercooked steak in a restaurant. Sometimes all that can be done is to take the deal this time and organize more effectively for the next round of bargaining. Always remember this: without fail, the stronger the union, the stronger the union contract.

different from votes you cast in other parts of your life. In state and national elections, we vote to elect someone else to do a job for us. In voting on a collective bargaining agreement, our vote obligates us to do certain things. We usually don't have the luxury of just voting "no" and then figuring that someone else will do what's needed to make things better. Chances are, the reason the bargaining team came back to the membership with what they did was because they got the best deal that seemed possible. So you usually will need to think of your vote to reject a tentative contract agreement as being a vote to get personally involved, so that the union will then have the extra clout needed to get a better settlement than what you just turned down.

If a contract is ratified, sometimes it takes a little while for the final language to get tidied up, and the new contract to be in place. Once it's printed, you should get a copy—which is your legal right—so you can know your workplace rights.

If a contract is voted down by the members, what next? Sometimes, the two sides will return to the bargaining table and try again to work out an acceptable deal. But sometimes they won't go back to negotiating, and a deadlock results.

What Happens If the Parties Deadlock?

Sometimes, the two sides can't reach agreement at the bargaining table on all the terms of a new contract. When this happens, a variety of mechanisms may kick in to determine the outcome. Sometimes, the parties call in a mediator, who is a neutral labor professional who works with both sides to try to find areas of acceptable compromise. If common ground can't be found, the union can call a strike in the hope that the employer's loss of production or ability to provide services to customers will force a softening of its bargaining position. On the employer side of the equation, it may seek to turn up the heat by closing the facility and "locking out" the workers, thereby cutting off their paychecks. Historically, disputes that develop this way have been resolved when one side or the other feels pressured enough to make additional compromises in order to reach an agreement.

What Happens in a Strike?

Private sector workers, and many public employees, have the right to strike. Usually, strikes are called either to get a first contract for a newly unionized workplace or to pressure the employer to agree to a more favorable settlement after a contract expires. (There are instances, although rare, where unions can use strikes while a contract is still in effect.) Unions do not decide lightly to call a strike. This decision is reached after an analysis of the situation and a strike vote by the members indicate that this is the most likely way for the workers' interests to prevail. If you do go out on strike, your union probably will provide at least partial strike pay, to ease the short-term economic impact. And you may live in a state where workers are eligible to collect unemployment compensation while they are out on strike.

Strikes are riskier than they used to be. In the past, it was pretty much par for the course that when a union needed to bring pressure to bear, it simply would "stop production"; that is, the members stopped working. As a practical matter, in a manufacturing setting this meant simply preventing Widget Company from continuing its widget production. In a service setting, the workers simply no longer provided services to customers or to the public. But as effective as strikes still can prove to be, in some industries changing technology has meant that it is increasingly difficult for unions simply to "stop production" in this way. (*The Washington Post*, for example, led the way in the 1970s into a new era of confrontational labor relations when it got around solid union picket lines outside its building by using helicopter pickups on its roof. And computer technology now makes it even easier for companies in the information industry to "produce" their product without workers on site.) Over the years, both private sector companies and public employers have become much more aggressive in their responses to strikes. Both have tried more and more to get rid of strikers and do what they can to continue to conduct business as usual.

Two Types of Strikes

The law in the private sector divides strikes into two categories. The first is economic strikes, consisting of the "garden variety" effort by unions to win a contract with more money and better working conditions. With respect to job rights in this context, the law makes a distinction that perhaps only a lawyer can fully appreciate: a company may not fire striking workers, but it may lawfully "permanently replace" them. (Many a "permanently replaced" worker has felt very much fired.) So unless the union can negotiate a wholesale return to work at the end of the strike, each striker is placed on a waiting list for future job vacancies as they arise.

The second category is what are known as unfair labor practice strikes. These are strikes that are triggered not by economic or contract demands of the union but by a union protest over certain unlawful actions taken by the company. ("Unfair labor practices" are violations of a federal law, and include such actions as firing a worker for union activism or for protesting health and safety violations.) In unfair labor practice strikes a company may hire substitute workers, but only on a temporary basis. Even if the union does not win the strike, if the union declares that the workers are ready to go back to their jobs, the company must take them back.

For public employees, often the services of a mediator or a fact-finder (someone who holds a mini-hearing where each side presents the facts and arguments to justify its bargaining positions) is required as a matter of law. And sometimes in the public sector, when the parties are unable to see eye to eye, an outside arbitrator (like a judge) or a government agency has the power to set the terms of what the new contract will be. Some public employees ultimately have the legal right to strike, but many don't. And some that don't have the legal right to strike routinely do so, anyway.

The Real Power: Away from the Table

Wouldn't the world be a wonderful place if those with better arguments, and the facts and right on their side, always won out? But just like much else in life, the outcome of contract negotiations is determined in large part simply by who has more power. Each side constantly evaluates during bargaining whether it can hold firm in its positions or whether it must com promise, based on its assessment of how much each side can exert pressure on the other if agreement is not reached.

49

Because of these power dynamics, effective union negotiators don't conceive of bargaining as taking place "in a vacuum." Throughout negotiations, unions that understand the big picture look for ways to demonstrate that the members stand behind their bargaining team. If an employer gets the message that the small group of union negotiators it's dealing with face to face is in fact speaking for large numbers of bargaining unit members, that can create enough pressure for the employer to give the union what it wants. Most important, the employer must believe that if issues aren't successfully resolved at the table, the members won't take the employer's "no" for an answer.

What this means is that if you want a good contract, you and your union may well not have the luxury of simply sending dedicated and skilled union negotiators off to deal with the employer and then waiting until they come back with a string of victories. Actions outside of the bargaining room may be necessary to get what's needed inside that room.

Contract Campaigns

Even as your negotiating team goes through the process of exchanging proposals with the employer, arguing them out, and seeing where acceptable resolutions can be found, you may be called upon to step forward and play a different type of role in the bargaining process. Your union may ask you and your co-workers to let the employer and perhaps also the public know, in a variety of ways, that the voice of the union negotiators is also your voice. The actions called for may be as simple as signing a petition supporting a contract demand or everyone wearing a certain color clothing or T-shirt on a "solidarity day" scheduled by the union. As things heat up, more assertive actions may be called for, like rallies on or off the worksite, conducting an informational picket before or after work at the employer's premises, or withholding your labor, either for a short period of time or in a full-blown strike. A pressure campaign against the employer that is fought on many fronts—a "contract campaign"—has been the key to union victory in many a contract fight.

Corporate Campaigns

In recent years, unions increasingly have turned to another way of waging a broader fight outside the bargaining room. These fights on a second front are referred to as corporate campaigns.

In a way, the "end game" in the bargaining process used to be pretty straightforward. If the parties didn't see eye to eye at the table, then economic pressure was brought to bear: either the union would strike or the employer would lock out the workers. The terms of the eventual contract settlement would be determined by how much each side felt the pain of the pocketbook.

But recent years have brought us negative developments in the law, shifts in the American (and world) economy, and the new technology that sometimes takes control of production out of the workers' hands. These have changed the union view of strikes. Now, unions often conclude that a strike is no longer necessarily the first resort, nor even the most powerful weapon in their arsenal.

So changing times and power relationships have launched the corporate campaign as a new form of union action.

In a corporate campaign, rather than just calling a strike, the union analyzes where the employer's weaknesses lie, and that's where it brings pressure to bear. A few examples:

♦ A hospital's business depends on how much confidence patients and potential patients have in its services; so the union may take out ads or run radio spots to publicize how understaffing affects the quality of care provided.

♦ An employer may rely very heavily on consumers viewing it as a good "corporate citizen," and may therefore be nervous about having its image tarnished; one newspaper union, for example, made a public point in bargaining of dramatizing that part-time workers (who received no company benefits) were forced to make ends meet by getting food stamps.

♦ A public agency needs continual funding from the legislature; so the union may collect and disclose examples of wasteful expenditures of tax-payer dollars by the agency.

In a given situation, creative pressure tactics may prove to be as effective, or even more so, than a traditional strike. If your union decides to go this route, you may be an essential part of the plan: collecting information about what's going on in the workplace, for example, or publicizing in the community information that the union has dug up on the employer.

51

The Legal Framework for Negotiations

The law doesn't dictate the specifics of what the parties must agree to in the course of negotiations. But various bargaining laws usually do set forth a framework for bargaining. Here are some of the basic legal principles.

Duty to Bargain in Good Faith

While laws do not force either side to agree to any particular proposal, they do require negotiators to approach bargaining with "a sincere resolve" to reach agreement. Agencies and courts that oversee bargaining won't stand in the way of negotiators taking firm positions and trying to get the other side to give at the table. But it's not enough to just go through the motions of bargaining. Each party must be willing to meet with the other at reasonable times and places, to be reasonably flexible in modifying positions, and to demonstrate in other ways that it is genuinely trying to reach agreement.

Subjects of Bargaining

Depending on the law covering your type of workplace, subjects of bargaining may be:

♦ "Mandatory," meaning that the parties must bargain over them if either side wants to. The covered topics are those dealing with "wages, hours, and other terms and conditions of employment," including health plans, pensions, leave policies, and so on.

♦ "Permissive" or "voluntary," meaning that either side has the right to decide not to bargain over that subject. Examples might be a proposal to change which employees are covered by the collective bargaining agreement, or one that addresses health and welfare or pension plans for retirees.

♦ "Non-negotiable" or illegal, meaning that the collective bargaining agreement cannot address that topic at all. The parties to a contract, for example, couldn't legally bargain over whether or not only union members can be hired.

The Right to Information

This is part of the framework of bargaining. In basic terms, the law says that if one party needs information to address issues to be discussed in negotiations, the other side must produce that information. (This right, by the way, also applies to information that's needed during the life of a contract to enforce its terms, such as when a union needs to get a look at employer records to pursue a grievance.)

Interest-Based Bargaining

Like most everything else in society, the dynamics of the labor relations process have changed quite a bit in recent years. The adversarial way that bargaining historically has been conducted has not been replaced, by any means. But one new model that is sometimes used is worth looking at.

Starting from some very different assumptions than those that form the basis of traditional negotiations, a relatively recent style of bargaining seeks to enable parties to reach agreement by using a new set of procedures. This form of negotiation goes by several different names: interest-based bargaining, mutual-gains bargaining, or sometimes "win-win."

The standard style of bargaining strongly resembles a game of poker. In a card game, it is understood by all that you are expected to hold your cards close to the vest; you've got no ethical or other obligation to let any of the other players know, in effect, where your strengths and weaknesses lie. In fact, the unwritten rules by which the game is played make it acceptable deliberately to mislead the other players by using such tactics as bluffing. Similar unspoken ground rules also dictate the behavior of the parties in a collective bargaining relationship. Outright lying may not be okay, but the nature of the adversarial relationship is such that a good deal of posturing is understood to be part of the way the game is played.

Negotiators in a standard bargaining relationship also need to possess many of the skills of good chess players. To make the series of decisions at a bargaining table about what items to trade off, and when to do so, a skillful negotiator must think ahead. What will the other sides' response be if I make this possible statement or take that possible action? And what options will those responses then leave me? This is the same type of strategizing that goes into a good game of chess.

As the standard bargaining process draws to a close, the dynamic between the parties often becomes more and more adversarial and confrontational. The process becomes increasingly tense as each side in effect "threatens" the other with what the consequences will be if agreement is not reached. Unions generally hold the "stick" of going out on strike or otherwise disrupting the orderly operation of the employer's enterprise, while employers have the potential leverage of locking out the workforce, or imposing regressive terms and conditions of employment (that is, making things worse than what the expiring contract provides).

A Different Bargaining Style

Interest-based bargaining, on the other hand, starts from some very different assumptions. This style of negotiation is based on the belief that the parties to a collective bargaining relationship have a joint interest in sharing information and in working together cooperatively to come up with mutually satisfactory resolutions to the issues before them. Because of the cooperation that underlies interest-based bargaining, negotiations that conclude successfully using this model often lead to a less confrontational and more productive relationship between the employer and the union long after the contract is signed.

In interest-based bargaining, all items on the bargaining table, from wages and fringe benefits to how work is to be done, are seen as problems to be solved creatively by the parties. The style by which this bargaining is conducted reflects these assumptions. For example, rather than having each bargaining team sit directly across from the other at the table, the seating is usually mixed. Fewer caucuses are taken, since the bargainers put more effort into brainstorming together to come up with possible solutions to problems than into crafting formal proposals and counter-proposals. And communications outside the bargaining room, both to union members and the public at large, are generally far less adversarial and strident in tone than what one generally sees in traditional bargaining.

When the union is dealing with an enlightened employer—that is, one genuinely seeking to reach a fair agreement with the union that will serve both parties' interests over time—interest-based bargaining can be an excellent tool. It can enable the union to get information that it might otherwise not have access to, and that information can point the way to new resolutions to stubborn problems. The negotiations process can be a highly efficient one, since the ground rules eliminate the need for most, if not all, posturing by the parties. And particularly in the public sector, where the formal scope of bargaining is usually more restrictive than in the private sector, an interest-based approach to a collective bargaining relationship can be a direct path to a seat at the table with the employer, so that the employees' voice can be heard on a wider range of issues.

Danger Can Lurk

But unions sometimes learn the hard way that interest-based bargaining can be filled with danger. Traditional bargaining, whatever its shortcomings, makes it clear which side is for and which side is against any particular proposal to change things in the workplace. The very nature of this style of bargaining means that the union has a great deal of incentive to keep its members aware of what's going on at the bargaining table. A completely uninformed membership is one unlikely to respond when called on to engage in a job action or another show of strength, should that prove necessary.

There are far too many examples in recent years of interest-based bargaining in which unions were not able to maintain sound footing. The mutual-gains approach does require an open atmosphere and sincere efforts toward a cooperative relationship. But unions sometimes forget that the membership simultaneously must be kept fully informed about what's happening at the bargaining table and what's at stake in the negotiations. Even as mutual and creative problem solving takes place at the table, the union leadership must take care to educate its members, so that they will be committed to taking the necessary action to confront the employer if that proves necessary. Mutual-gains bargaining, of course, doesn't always work. So unions need to do the necessary groundwork so that if settlement is not reached, it will be possible to shift gears on short notice and take on the employer in a real contract fight.

YOUR

union contract:

WHAT IT COVERS

If you don't already have one, it's worth getting your own copy

of the union contract. Depending on what bargaining law you're covered by, you're probably legally entitled to get a copy from your local union. Don't try to read the collective bargaining agreement cover to cover: unless your social life is very, very empty, it's extremely unlikely that you'll find the entire "union book" gripping reading. But it's worth checking out the table of contents and at least skimming the agreement. You'll probably find that there's much more covered in it than you suspected. You may discover that you have more rights than you realized and the potential for more control over your working life.

What's covered and what's not covered in a collective bargaining agreement varies quite a bit, depending on a lot of factors. Both what legally may be included in the contract and what the contract terms will be on particular subjects are determined by such factors as what bargaining law governs your workplace, the sort of work you do, and what the standard practices are in your industry or geographic area. The discussion below covers items that are "typical" for union contracts. Keep in mind, though, that every contract is pretty much unique, and that not every workplace rule or agreement is contained in the collective bargaining agreement.

The Essentials: Pay, Benefits and More

Collective bargaining agreements almost always cover the basic dollars-and-cents issues that people think of when they think of a unionized workplace: all aspects of pay, health coverage and other benefits, different types of leave, and the like. (But here's one big example of the differences you'll find from one type of contract to another: you may discover that your contract does not cover some of the basic economic aspects of your workplace life because, particularly if you are in the public sector, pay levels and certain benefits may be decided by law or through another process besides union negotiations.)

Payday Variations

On items like pay, you may be surprised at the level of detail in the contract. You may find, for example, page after page after page spelling out eligibility for different pay levels, rules for shift or other differentials, when and how you can get a raise, and when—and if!—your pay can be cut. The contract may even specify what information is to appear on your pay stub, how frequently you are to be paid (perhaps even when you are entitled to receive your money when the normal payday falls on a holiday), and rules concerning direct bank deposit of your pay.

It's common to see different union contracts tackle the same topic in a variety of ways. But the subject of pay determination may be the area in which union contracts display the greatest number of approaches.

Some contracts set forth specific dollar amounts, payable on an hourly or other basis. Under such a setup, all employees performing a particular type of work or all those with certain seniority must be paid at the same rate. Other contracts provide for a base salary, but they also provide for the possibility of "merit pay" or other variables that can vary the pay levels for individual employees.

For some types of work, it's common for the collective bargaining agreement to set only a minimum salary for each classification. Under such a setup, the employer may not pay less than that amount but is free to pay anyone more. Or, particularly in direct sales jobs and in the food service industry, compensation may consist of a contractually specified base rate plus a formula for commission or provision for tips.

And some contracts set up a two-tier pay system, with newly hired employees coming in at a lower rate and working up a different pay scale. Sometimes, but not always, after a certain number of years these employees catch up in pay to their longer term co-workers.

Finally, there is also the device of "grandfathering." (Use of the term "grand-parenting" has not yet caught on.) "Grandfathered" or "red-circled"employees are those who, despite some change in their job or even the elimination of an entire classification, are entitled to hold on to their old pay rates.

Schedules and Benefits

Your work schedule may well be covered in great detail as well. There may be very specific language dictating who can be assigned or who can choose to work on particular days or times, along with pay levels attached to night, weekend or holiday shifts. Supplementing laws already on the books, your contract may define "overtime" and regulate its use/abuse and any extra compensation that comes into play. Depending on the type of work that you do, your contract may guarantee a certain amount of time to get ready to begin work or to wash up at the end of a shift, may define and specify compensation for being "on call" or for traveling to a particular worksite, or may set mileage reimbursement levels or per diem rates for travel.

There may well be a similar level of detail for benefits. Sometimes an appendix to the contract will list what's covered and what's not in the health care plan, life insurance and disability policies, and other benefits.

Many other "essentials" are covered in almost every contract. Here are some that frequently appear.

Holidays and Leave

Your contract probably spells out what holidays are observed. It also will outline the various types of leave—sick and vacation, perhaps parental and bereavement leave, even time off for jury duty—saying how much you're entitled to and under what circumstances, and detailing procedures you may have to follow to use your leave. You may discover that there are types of leave contained in the union contract—such as the option of taking unpaid time off or adjusting your work schedule so that you can go back to school—that are used so seldom you weren't even aware of them.

Job Security

Nearly every collective bargaining agreement contains provisions on the discipline of employees. And this is not surprising, since there is really no other aspect of employment where the difference between those who are protected

"IT'S NOT IN HERE!"

Suppose you actually read through your entire union contract, and don't find a particular topic covered that is of interest to you. What might the explanation be, and what can you do about it?

It's possible that the item you're interested in has in fact been addressed by the union and the employer but in a document elsewhere. There may be language on the subject in an employee handbook or other company policy, or in a regulation or statute. Or it may be found in a written memorandum of understanding or other agreement reached by your union and employer, but one that was not included in the printed contract booklet.

And the concept of "past practice" may create enforceable rights that an arbitrator will read into a collective bargaining agreement, even if there is no specific language in the contract that spells out those practices.

So the first thing you should do is simply ask your union steward for information.

You may learn, of course, that items of importance to you are not in fact covered by the contract or by another written agreement enforceable by the union. There may be a variety of explanations if this is the case: some topics simply, as a matter of law, may not be included in the contract; or your union may have tried in earlier rounds of bargaining to win certain contract language, but without success; or it may be that particular items never made it to the proposal stage in bargaining, because the bargaining committee and union leadership just weren't aware that those topics were of concern to members, or because they didn't set as high a priority on them as you believe they should have.

No matter what the reason for a topic not being covered by the contract, communication is the order of the day. Asking why something is not included may give you the explanation you need as to where else to look, or why the item can't be addressed in negotiations.

Even if nothing can be done to address your concern at the moment, your inquiry may be a valuable source of input to your union, which needs to know how the contract bargaining process can be put to better use in the future to serve the interests of the members.

by a union contract and those who are not is more dramatic. A fundamental doctrine of American law is known as "employment at will." Stripped to its essentials, this means that an employer is within its legal rights if it undertakes disciplinary action or termination for no reason—or even a bad reason. Even if an employer's action is clearly arbitrary, unreasonable, or unfair, "employees at will" have no legal recourse. If you don't have the coverage of a union contract, the only protections you have come from laws or policies that are limited in scope, such as anti-discrimination statutes.

But don't be surprised if you see that your contract does not spell out what particular infractions may lead to discipline or what penalty is applied to particular acts of misconduct. Many contracts simply say that there is a "just cause" or "good cause" standard for dealing out discipline. Don't worry; these words mean a lot more than you might think. They are what are known as terms of art, meaning that they have acquired some fairly precise meanings through the history of your workplace, and through arbitration or court decisions. Rather than attempting to write what would be a pretty thick book, specifying each and every possible infraction, and all the different circumstances that might surround it, most unions and employers simply use this kind of contractual shorthand. Each case is then decided on its own merits, but with the facts at hand being evaluated in light of the standards that have developed over time.

Even if the particular infractions that you can be disciplined for are not specified in the contract, there may well be some specific guidelines that are set out. For example, it is common for a contract to require that progressive discipline must be followed. This means that ordinarily there must be a series of infractions to justify increasingly severe punishment. So the first time you come in late without notifying your supervisor, you may well receive only a spoken or written warning. But if you persist in the same conduct, or engage in other misconduct, on each subsequent occasion your employer might well be justified in escalating the penalty, to the point of suspension and eventually termination. (But don't get too creative and try to argue that just because this was only the first time you slugged a co-worker, you can't be terminated on the spot.)

A related concept is that "the punishment must fit the crime." Through either general or specific language, the contract will usually make it clear that if there's been only a minor infraction there can be only a minor penalty. So if you're a few minutes late to work a couple of times, the employer couldn't get away with trying to fire you for this.

Your collective bargaining agreement is quite likely to cover the procedures that must be followed if your employer wishes to discipline you. Specifying such procedures is a way of making sure that there is a measure of "due process," a concept that covers basic notions of fairness.

For example, your contract may well require that your employer put in writing whatever misconduct or deficiencies in performance it alleges. This serves as the equivalent of a formal complaint or indictment in a court proceeding; it's only fair that you be told what you allegedly have done wrong, so that you can adequately defend yourself. You'll see that your contract probably goes on to provide for some opportunity—either in a meeting or by submitting something in writing—to challenge the allegations against you. Whether spelled out in the contract itself or in a law, your union has the right to be given documents and other information that relate to any charges against you. This may even cover information relating to your co-workers. If, for example, part of your defense is that you are being singled out for harsher punishment than that given out to other employees, your union will be able to obtain the records of others who committed similar infractions.

And should your employer not back off, the resulting disciplinary action can be reviewed through the formal grievance/arbitration procedure, covered in Chapters 7 and 8.

Who Is Covered

Your union contract will not cover everyone in your workplace. Probably on the first page or so, you'll find the definition of the bargaining unit and jurisdiction covered. Whether the boundaries of contract coverage are based on type of work performed, location, or other factors, the agreement itself will set forth who's covered and who's not. And with technology and other factors transforming American workplaces at a rapid pace, your contract may even specify how it is to be determined whether new types of work that come into existence will or won't be covered by the terms of the contract.

Membership and Dues

Your contract will specify what requirements there may be, and what procedures must be followed, for joining or quitting the union, or for paying dues or fees to the union. Most workplaces nowadays provide for dues checkoff—that is, a procedure for having your dues deducted directly from your pay. Your contract will include the procedures that apply to this process as well.

Probationary Period

Your contract is likely to specify what probationary period applies when new employees are hired. This is the period in which an employer is permitted to terminate an employee with little or no justification. Probationary periods can run from as little as thirty days for some less skilled work to a full seven years for college professors.

Job Reductions

The contract will also set the criteria under which your employer can cut hours or lay off employees. For example, it may be necessary for the employer to prove that there is a "compelling business necessity" to justify any shrinking of the workforce. And the contract will cover how it is determined which employees get to keep their jobs and which don't. (This is often determined by seniority, that is, length of service with the employer.) There may be detailed procedures including such items as how much notice must be given, determination of severance pay, retraining rights, and priority for being rehired in the future.

Retirement Options

In addition to whatever regular pension plan or alternative tax-deferred plan may be in place, the contract may provide for other options. For example, you may find that once you reach a certain age, or have been with the employer long enough, you may have the right to have a "phased retirement," meaning that you can choose to have a reduced work schedule. Or the contract may allow "buyouts," permitting certain employees to leave with either a cash settlement or a reduced retirement payout.

Health and Safety

Adding to legal protections that are on the books for all employees, your collective bargaining agreement may contain rights for your workplace. Some contracts contain only a general statement that health and safety standards will be respected. This is a more valuable provision than it may at first appear to be. This is because such contract language gives the union the right to challenge lax health and safety standards through the grievance/arbitration procedure, rather than having to go outside to a separate agency to try to enforce the law.

Joint Committees

Often, contracts set up joint labor-management committees. These are sometimes given specific responsibilities, like monitoring health and safety conditions in the workplace or changes in healthcare benefits. But some joint committees are given full authority to address any matters of concern, whether or not these items are covered elsewhere in the contract or even are negotiable under law.

Union Institutional Rights

Most contracts contain language providing the tools the union needs to conduct its day-to-day operations: time off needed by stewards to represent members, access to the worksite by union representatives, use of the employer's bulletin boards for union notices, and similar guarantees.

Personnel Records

In addition to (or buried deep within) the contract language covering discipline you may find that you have the right as an individual to review whatever documents have been placed in your personnel file or to submit rebuttal statements to be included in your file.

Duration

Printed right on the cover, or near the end of the contract, you'll find the duration clause. This tells you how long the contract will remain in effect (usually measured in years, and often three years or less). Sometimes the contract itself spells out under what circumstances its terms will be extended after it expires. You may also find language setting forth the time frames or procedures the parties have agreed to for bargaining the next contract.

And Even More

You'll find many other topics covered in the contract. It may, for example, provide for substance abuse or other counseling services. It may tell you when and where you are allowed to smoke. It may set standards for personal appearance in the workplace, or rules that apply to wearing name badges or identifying yourself by name to customers, co-workers or the public.

This book can't tell you exactly which provisions are in your contract; it can guarantee, however, that if you read your union contract you'll find things you never knew were there!

Remember: The Union Contract Is a Living Document

Generally, when the parties sign off on a new collective bargaining agreement, they are agreeing to be bound by its terms until a new agreement takes its place some years later. But it's still worth asking your steward about changes you might like to see before then, since there are a couple of exceptions to this general rule.

First, your contract may provide for the kind of joint labor-management committee mentioned above. If this is the case, your union may be able to use such a committee to address your concern. Or sometimes collective bargaining agreements themselves will provide that some of their terms are up for renegotiation during the life of the contract. The most typical instance is pay during the later years of a contract, but sometimes other events—such as the introduction of new technology—trigger contract provisions that give your union the right to bargain.

In addition—even if the contract itself doesn't specifically spell this out—quite often the union has the right to bargain over changes that the employer wants to make during the life of a contract. For example, it may be that your employer cannot decide to relocate or to reduce the workforce without first giving the union the opportunity to bargain.

grievances:

ENFORCING WORKPLACE LAW

Virtually every union contract contains a grievance/arbitration procedure, which is the way the union and the employer tackle disagreements about workplace rights covered by the contract. Filing a grievance is the equivalent of starting a lawsuit: you put in writing what you believe another party has done that is contrary to the law, and what action will be necessary to correct the situation. If after going through a series of procedural steps the dispute is not resolved, then the last step of the grievance process—arbitration—is the equivalent of appearing before a judge to argue the case out and obtain a final resolution, one way or the other.

What Grievances Can Cover

A grievance is not a device for curing whatever ails you; your contract itself will have a definition of what is and is not covered by the grievance procedure. The most favorable definition of the scope of a grievance—though not the most common one—gives you the right to use the contract grievance procedure to challenge any area of concern connected to your workplace life. More commonly, a griev-

A NOTE OF CAUTION: INSUBORDINATION

You may find yourself being told by your supervisor to do something that he or she has no right to insist on under the union contract. The natural temptation is to say, "I know my rights, I'm not doing it!"

But be forewarned about the "work, then grieve" rule. This is the generally accepted notion in the world of labor relations that you do not have the right to disobey an employer directive, even if that directive is in violation of the collective bargaining agreement. The required response is to do what the employer says, under protest, and then to pursue relief through the grievance procedure. While there are exceptions—such as for dangerous health and safety violations—think twice before risking discipline for insubordination.

ance will be defined in a more narrow fashion, covering at most only challenges to specific provisions in the contract.

And quite often, the contract will provide that not all of its terms are subject to challenge through the grievance procedure. Sometimes, as a matter of either law or policy, you will be required to seek relief somewhere else. For example, if you have a problem with how a health insurance provider has treated you, you will most likely find that there is a complaint procedure outside of the contract that you will be required to use. Or you may find that even if your collective bargaining agreement contains language prohibiting certain types of personnel actions, the contract itself may require you to go to a government agency to enforce your rights.

There can be another type of exclusion from what is covered by the grievance procedure. Sometimes, because of the way a bargaining law is written or simply as a matter of power at the bargaining table, your employer may have been able to exclude certain matters from being grieved at all. These are often areas of what are termed "management rights," that is, matters considered to be enough within the prerogative of the employer that they may not be challenged under the union contract's grievance procedure.

Finally, you may find that while some disputes under the contract may be processed through the steps of the grievance procedure, they cannot be taken all the way to arbitration.

Who Can File a Grievance

Individual members of the bargaining unit—that is, you and your co-workers—can initiate grievances under the contract if you believe that the terms of the collective bargaining agreement have been violated. In fact, the law covering your type of workplace may even provide that you have the right to initiate a grievance with your employer without a union representative even being present. But keep a few things in mind if you consider this course of action. First, the law provides that the union must be given the opportunity to be present at any "adjustment" (that is, a settlement) of a grievance. Second, as we will see when we discuss arbitration, past a certain level it is almost always your union, not you as an individual, that has the right to pursue the grievance. And perhaps most important, for your own protection and for the good of your co-workers, it's almost always a good idea to involve your union representative right from the very beginning of pursuing a grievance.

Unions themselves also initiate grievances. As the exclusive representative of everyone in the bargaining unit, the union has the right—and, quite often, also the legal obligation—to use the collective bargaining agreement to challenge the employer's improper or unfair actions. The union will sometimes file grievances over employer conduct that affects everyone in the bargaining unit—for example, if a unilateral employer directive limits everyone's ability to take leave days. The union may also file grievances on behalf of one particular group of employees, such as workers on one shift who are denied proper pay. And there is a third possibility: sometimes the union finds it necessary or politically desirable to initiate a grievance on behalf of a single individual. (This may be a useful way to provide some "protection" to that individual, or perhaps to send a message to the employer that the union stands firmly behind this one employee.)

Although this is not always the case, it may be that your employer also has the right to file grievances under the contract. In a way, this is fair. Since the collective bargaining agreement is a set of rules that all those in the workplace are required to live by, it makes some sense for any individual or group in the workplace—including the employer—to be able to challenge what it believes are violations of the rules.

Why Grieve?

The natural inclination is to think about pursuing a grievance only if it looks like it has a reasonably good chance of coming up a winner. Why file a grievance in the first place, unless your union is determined to take the case all the way to arbitration if the employer doesn't back down?

There may be lots of good reasons for a union to file a grievance that it doesn't expect to "win."

Fire a Warning Shot

There are times when it doesn't make sense to think about fighting the employer to the death on a particular action. It may just not be worth it to arbitrate a relatively minor erosion of existing working conditions, or what looks like a one-time event. At the same time, rather than do nothing, a group grievance could serve to put the employer on notice that its action has not gone unnoticed, and that if it tries the same maneuver again, it may well have a serious fight on its hands.

Shine a Light

One of the most frustrating experiences in the life of a union representative is to hear an employer say, "That's just you complaining; none of the people you say you represent even cares." Sometimes it takes a grievance filed by an employee—or two or three or more—to get the employer to acknowledge that a particular problem is real and needs to be addressed.

Build a Record

One not entirely humorous definition of paranoia is "a heightened appreciation of reality." Sometimes it's hard to know where to draw a line between an isolated memo taking you to task for something and the first deadly serious shot in your supervisor's war against you. If there may be a suspension or termination action looming in your future, sometimes the wisest course of action is to begin to build a written record in your defense now.

Forge Employee Unity

It may well be that, for one reason or another, an immediate practical resolution of a particular problem may not be in the cards. But a grievance—

particularly a group grievance—might be just what is needed to start building solidarity among those wronged by a particular supervisor or policy. If you and others can get it together enough to take a small action, like filing a grievance, this may be the first step toward you and your co-workers later doing whatever it takes to fight—and win—on this or a bigger issue.

An Overview of the Grievance Procedure

All grievance procedures require going through a series of steps, with the contract itself identifying when each step is to take place, what precisely is to occur, and who may or must be involved at each stage of the process. Generally, the procedures get more formal as you go through each of the steps. Some grievances are resolved successfully at the earlier stages of the process, while others are not pursued past a certain point for a variety of reasons. Before we take a look at what the steps of the grievance procedure look like, here are a few notes of caution.

First, if you read through the grievance procedures contained in your collective bargaining agreement, some of it may look like fairly technical stuff. You'll probably find requirements as to the format that must be followed in writing up grievances, the rules for who receives certain grievance filings, calculation of time frames for processing a grievance (such as the difference between "working days" and "calendar days"), and the like. Don't be intimidated by any of this; your union steward has received training in how to process grievances and has additional help to call on if needed. The best advice for you is, don't try to wing it on your own! As soon as something happens that you think might properly be challenged through the grievance procedure, consult with your steward.

Second, you are to be commended if you familiarize yourself with the provisions of your contract. But don't automatically assume that, because of what looks like plain language in the contract, there is nothing that can be done to deal with a workplace problem that you have. Sometimes even the plain English in a contract doesn't mean what it says. (Or, as the question was put by the Marx Brothers, "Who you gonna believe, me or your own eyes?") For example, you may be able to count well enough for it to seem completely clear that too many days have gone by since a particular event occurred for you to meet the time frame set forth in the contract for initiating a grievance. But it's worth at least consulting with your steward, since you may learn that there are sometimes unwritten exceptions even to such seemingly clear-cut provisions, such as the grievance time clock stopping for holidays. Or you may learn that there are other mechanisms, besides the grievance procedure, that can be used to address the problem.

And third, don't make the mistake of assuming that it would be useless to pursue a grievance, because you think you'd never be able to get enough evidence to prove your case. The fact is, both your contract and the law probably give your union the right to obtain vast quantities of documents and other information from your employer, if that information is needed to evaluate a potential or pending grievance. So if proof of your grievance over unfair treatment lies in determining how your employer has dealt with co-workers under circumstances similar to yours, your union will probably be able to get hold of the relevant personnel records.

The Steps of a Grievance

Before just about any workplace complaint is put into writing an attempt should be made to work through the problem at the lowest level. Even if your contract's grievance procedure doesn't specifically call for an informal, oral step to start out with, you and/or your union steward should talk to a supervisor in an attempt to clear up any misunderstandings, or to resolve any disagreement. This is almost always a good idea, in part because once a complaint is committed to writing, parties' positions tend to harden. And even if an informal attempt to address a problem does not in fact resolve it, it generally has the beneficial effect of clarifying what the problem is and how the parties may see it differently.

But if informal attempts don't work, the next step consists of formally putting the grievance in writing. The contract may require a certain amount of detail here, such as identifying the specific contract provisions that you allege have been violated. But generally the idea is simply to lay out, at least in general terms, that an identified action taken by the employer is being challenged, and that certain relief is sought. Your contract booklet itself may contain a sample form to be used to initiate a grievance.

One or more face-to-face meetings take place following the filing of a formal written grievance. At each stage, the participants on each side generally will be higher up in each organization's "food chain," and each meeting will get a little more formal than the one before it. At these meetings, the union and employer representatives try to hash out whether they agree on what the facts are, whether the contract has in fact been violated, and if so, what it will take to resolve the grievance. The employer usually is required to furnish the union with a written statement after each meeting, setting forth its position. If the union chooses to kick the grievance up to the next step, it likewise generally is required to do this in writing.

Your Role in the Process

What is your role in processing a grievance through the steps? First, of course, it is your job initially to approach your union representative and report the problem as you see it. You will need to set forth the facts as accurately as you can and to make sure that your representative understands not only what has happened, but why it is a matter of concern to you and, perhaps, your co-workers as well. As the grievance case goes on, your steward or union grievance committee may well need additional information to evaluate or to process the grievance. Since you have a stake in the outcome, you should be prepared to assist them in obtaining any needed information. Building a winning grievance case usually is a team effort.

A number of factors, having to do with the specific procedures in your contract and with the labor relations process in general, will dictate whether it is advisable or even possible for you to attend grievance meetings. There may be reasons, such as the danger of an unhelpful personality clash between you and a supervisor, for it to be a wiser course of action for you not to be present at a particular meeting. But generally, you can and should play a positive role by attending a grievance meeting. Factual matters may come up during the meeting that you are in the best position to evaluate and to respond to. And besides, this is your "day in court," so it makes sense for you to be able to observe firsthand what is being said.

That said, keep in mind that a careful balance must be maintained between you and your union representatives in processing a grievance. Most likely, you are the person in the best position to know the facts and the real-life impact of the employer's actions on you and your co-workers. At the same time, when it comes to labor relations matters such as processing a grievance, your union representative has been trained to do the job. So usually what makes most sense at a grievance meeting is for you to play a support role and let your union representative take the lead in presenting and arguing the grievance. But this doesn't mean that you should be a passive onlooker, by any means. Both you and your union representatives have an obligation to set aside whatever time is needed before and after meetings with the employer to go over the case. Take whatever time is needed to discuss what has happened so far and to plan the next steps.

Relief Available Under the Grievance Procedure

An important consideration in deciding whether and how to pursue any grievance is the question of what you can get if you win. Though the language of your contract's grievance procedure will determine in large part what relief can be obtained by filing a grievance, it's useful to understand that there are certain general categories of remedies.

Perhaps the most clear-cut type of relief that can be obtained through the grievance procedure is in those cases where one or more individuals have suffered a direct and measurable financial harm. For example, if a two-week suspension is overturned, a "make whole" remedy will include payment of lost wages and restoration of any benefits (such as payment into a retirement plan, or accrual of leave). There may also be nonfinancial consequences that can be remedied through the grievance procedure, such as cleaning up the employee's personnel file by deleting references to the suspension.

In grievances that challenge an employer action such as the improper issuance of a new workplace policy, a successful resolution would include withdrawing that policy. If your employer takes an action that is in violation of a provision of the contract, appropriate relief might include an agreement that similar employer actions will not take place in the future.

For all sorts of reasons, it is in both parties' interests for an employer and a union to work together successfully to resolve a pending grievance. For one thing, creative solutions can often be devised by those most familiar with the situation, and this can pave the way for everyone ending up satisfied with the outcome. By contrast, when a case goes all the way to an arbitrator for a hearing and a final decision, the types of relief that are possible are usually fairly restricted. It is not uncommon for the contract itself to set certain limits on what the arbitrator has the power to order, such as limiting the arbitrator's ability to reduce the penalty in a disciplinary action.

And even if your union contract itself does not contain restrictions on what constitutes appropriate relief, there are commonly accepted limitations on the authority of arbitrators. For example, arbitrators cannot award "punitive damages" or damages for "pain and suffering," which you would often be able to get in civil litigation. (But before you start thinking, "To heck with the grievance procedure, I'll just go to court," be forewarned that quite often the law says that an aggrieved party is required to go through the grievance process rather than just filing a lawsuit.)

Finally, any time the final resolution of a dispute is placed in the hands of a third party, there is the risk of ending up with a decision that "cuts the baby in half," perhaps awkwardly enough that neither side to the dispute walks away satisfied.

Contract Creativity: Tactical Uses of Grievances

Creative unionists keep in mind the importance of not only the content of a grievance but how a grievance is filed and pursued. With a bit of thought about the underlying dynamics in a workplace, the union can use the filing of a grievance as a tactical tool, to educate and mobilize members, or to send a message to the employer.

Let's consider first the format used to file a grievance. Suppose that an employer has denied requests for approved leave submitted by a number of employees. The union believes that this violates a provision in the contract, and it decides to challenge the employer. One possibility—the most obvious one—is for the union itself to file a single grievance on behalf of all those affected by the employer's action. Procedurally, this results in the employer having to respond one time, to one grievance, as it deals with the union as the party pursuing the grievance.

But there are other possible ways to pursue such a matter. The union might choose, for example, to initiate a group grievance, with individual employees each signing the initial written grievance. Attacking the problem this way can have the advantage of promoting a sense of participation on the part of each individual who actually puts pen in hand and signs. And the necessity of getting individual signatures from each employee affected means that the union has to reach out and explain to each employee why the employer's action violates the collective bargaining agreement, and that the union is doing something about it. Finally, consider the difference in these two methods of pursuing this grievance from the point of view of the employer. A grievance signed individually by a number of employees sends a clear message to the employer that its response will be observed and evaluated not just by the union as an organization but by real-life members, too.

Now consider yet a third possible way to pursue such a grievance: a mass filing of grievances. A very effective tactic to put pressure on an employer is for the union to organize a large number of employees to each file an individual grievance on a particular matter. This results in a much bigger expenditure of time and effort on the employer's part, as it is forced to indi-

75

vidually process numerous grievances. And it may send the clearest message of all that there is a problem to be dealt with, and that that problem has been identified as such by a great many individuals, not "just the union."

And there are creative ways to process a grievance through the procedural steps so as to involve and educate members as well as put pressure on the employer. For example, many contracts contain provisions authorizing a grievant to be released from normal work duties to prepare for or to participate in grievance meetings with the employer. So if the union has chosen to file a large number of individual grievances, rather than one grievance covering all the affected individuals, the employer will have to contend with releasing quite a few people from their normal work assignments.

Or at an even earlier stage, your contract may provide that you are to meet with your immediate supervisor to discuss a potential grievance, even before the grievance is reduced to writing. In this instance, there can be immediate pressure brought to bear on the employer if a large number of individuals chooses the same moment to stop doing their regular work because they need to talk to their supervisors about a potential grievance.

Direct Action: Better Than a Grievance?

There's no question that the ability to use the grievance/arbitration procedure to challenge employer violations of the terms of the collective bargaining agreement is one of the most potent weapons in the union arsenal. Every day, American unions successfully use contractual grievance procedures to win back the jobs of fired members, to protect wages and benefits, to prevent employers from closing down entire workplaces, and much else. Obtaining relief through pursuing a grievance, perhaps all the way to arbitration, is less costly, less risky, and less disruptive than if the union had to go to court or lead its members out on a strike.

But as effective and efficient as grievance procedures can be, the advantages are often accompanied by a number of disadvantages: the long time it often takes to resolve the dispute, the cost in union dollars and time to fight cases, and the shifting of direct control over the problem and its resolution from the affected employees to union officials, staffers, and attorneys.

Because of the drawbacks that can accompany the use of a grievance procedure, sometimes employees and their unions are better off if they can take direct action to force a wayward employer to mend its ways. Especially with a cynical employer, one who may count on the passage of time or the limited relief available through a grievance procedure working in its favor, what's needed is a direct, quick, "in your face" demonstration of the employees' will.

Take, for example, the all too common situation of an employer determined to remove work being done by unionized employees from the protections of the union contract. In one case, a company sought to contract out the cafeteria work in its building to a non-union company and to cast off the unionized workers. The workers' union might well have had a strong grievance challenging the employer's move to throw its members out on the street, and a year or so later might have gotten an arbitrator to rule in its favor. But the unionized employees in the building came up with a much quicker and more dramatic way to demonstrate to the employer that its planned actions would have serious consequences: everyone (except for managers, of course) stopped buying food in the cafeteria. The message to the employer was clear and immediate: unless you reach an acceptable accommodation with us as to who's going to work in this cafeteria, this cafeteria isn't going to do much business! The employer got the message, and all of the cafeteria workers stayed on the company payroll.

arbitration:

THE END OF THE LINE

Though it's best to resolve workplace disputes at the lowest level possible—to save time and money, and to avoid uncertainty—quite often no resolution is possible by the last step of the grievance procedure. So you may find yourself at the end of the line: arbitration.

While each of the meetings that takes place at the various steps of the grievance procedure is sort of a mini–"day in court," an arbitration hearing is pretty much the real thing. An arbitrator is a neutral third party, usually an attorney, selected jointly by the employer and the union. Professional arbitrators function much as judges do in regular courts of law. Arbitrators swear in witnesses, rule on who can testify and on what evidence can be introduced. The payment for the arbitrator's services, and certain other costs associated with the process, usually are split fifty-fifty by the employer and the union.

A private organization, the American Arbitration Association, and a federal agency, the Federal Mediation and Conciliation Service, are two organizations that provide lists of qualified arbitrators to unions and employers. Usually a new arbitrator is selected to hear each arbitration case, but sometimes the parties to a collective bargaining relationship will use a set group of "permanent arbitrators" or "umpires," to hear all arbitration cases. And sometimes an arbitration board hears a case, with one neutral arbitrator joined by two others: one appointed by the union, the other by the employer.

Almost always, the arbitrator has the authority to make a final decision that is binding on both parties. This makes the right to go to arbitration an extremely powerful weapon in the union's arsenal. Unlike the steps of the grievance procedure, in which a series of close-minded employer representatives can "just say no," the employer knows that at the end of an arbitration proceeding, there will be a final, enforceable determination.

But be aware that in some instances, spelled out in the union contract, only advisory arbitration takes place. This means that the arbitrator has the power only to issue a recommendation to the parties; since an award of this type does not have the force of law, enforcement rests with whatever forces of persuasion and agitation the union and its members can bring to bear.

In some ways, an arbitration proceeding is an even more powerful tool for the union than a courtroom trial would be. For one thing, resolving a dispute through arbitration is almost always quicker, easier, and less expensive than taking a case to court. For another, unlike a judge's decision, there are usually fewer opportunities for an employer unhappy with the ruling of an arbitrator to challenge that ruling or to have it overturned on appeal. And consequently, there are fewer opportunities available for an employer who believes that "justice delayed is justice denied, and that's a good thing" deliberately to delay the final resolution of a dispute.

What to Expect If Your Grievance Is Going to Hearing

If your case goes all the way to arbitration, you can expect that some time—usually measured in months—will pass between the employer's final rejection of the grievance and the actual arbitration hearing. Some of this delay is unavoidable, since often the employer and the union will have to go through an agreed upon process to select an arbitrator and to set a hearing date that will fit everyone's schedule.

But participants in the process can put that time to good use for preparation. Just as with processing a grievance through the steps of the grievance procedure, there may well be the need for intensive investigation of the facts to get ready for the hearing. You may need to locate witnesses to any disputed events or to track down the history of other occurrences that may factor into your case. And you, or others who may be called to testify at the arbitration hearing, will need to prepare to give testimony.

And the representatives of both sides and the arbitrator will have work to do in advance of the hearing. Your representative, for example, may be trying to get documents or other evidence from the other side, to help build your case. And the arbitrator may be pushing both sides to define the issues to be presented to the arbitrator for resolution and to determine what witnesses will be testifying and which documents may be admitted as evidence.

The Arbitration Process

If you've got a basic idea of what takes place in a courtroom trial, you've also got a fairly good notion of what to expect at an arbitration hearing. The major difference is that arbitrations are conducted in a less formal way than court proceedings. For example, you'll never see an arbitrator wearing a judge's robe.

Be prepared for the remote possibility that your union would prefer not to have you present at the hearing, for a variety of reasons. Although this is unlikely, it may come up. So take it upon yourself to work out, well in advance of the hearing, whether you will be in attendance. Since it is your "day in court," you should agree not to attend only if you are satisfied that the union has a legitimate reason to make such a request.

Assuming that you will be present, here's an overall view of what you can expect on the day of the arbitration hearing.

The Hearing

The hearing itself will take place in a regular meeting room of some sort, with the arbitrator sitting either at a separate table up front or at the head of a large conference table. Those on the union side—you, perhaps one or more stewards or grievance officials, and whoever is serving as the union's representative—will sit together, as will a similarly composed group from the employer's side. There may also be an official court reporter, who will be producing a transcript of the proceedings for the use of both parties and the arbitrator.

After some preliminary matters—such as determining what witnesses and evidence will be presented—are determined, the formal hearing will begin. Depending on the type of case, either the union or the employer will

YOUR ROLE IN ARBITRATION

At all stages of the grievance/arbitration process, your role is to assist your union representatives in pursuing and processing the case. It's not enough simply to file a grievance and then figure that the union will do the necessary work to win it. As a very practical matter, you are likely to be familiar with facts that your union representatives are not, so you need to stay involved at all stages so that you can provide important input. You also owe it to yourself and to the union to be involved every step of the way, so that you can have a realistic outlook if the question of settlement comes up at any stage of the processing of the case.

At the arbitration hearing itself, the human dynamics can get a little tricky. The last thing you want is for the other side or the arbitrator to get the impression that you and the union representatives are not completely in sync. So make sure that you understand pretty clearly what is going to take place at the hearing before you enter the room. Work this out with your representative, but usually it will be preferable for you to write notes during the hearing itself, rather than try to talk to your representative, which is likely to be too distracting. There will be plenty of breaks during the day during which you can talk things over.

Keep in mind that it is natural for it to take a fair amount of time to complete the arbitration process. And even after the "final and binding" arbitration award is issued, either party to a case may pursue an appeal. Sometimes an appeal is simply one more item in an employer's bag of tricks to delay and add unnecessary expense to the union's pursuit of justice.

So while you have every right to be insistent about being informed about the progress of your case, you also have an obligation to be reasonable in your expectations about how quickly it will be resolved.

go first in presenting its case, beginning with an opening statement in which the representative outlines what the case is all about. Usually, witnesses testify under oath, first on direct examination (that is, they answer questions asked by the representative of the party calling the witness) and then on cross examination. The arbitrator, too, may choose to ask questions.

Periodically, the arbitrator may need to resolve some procedural or other matter, or for another reason may go "off the record." This means that the court reporter will take a break, and there will be no official transcript of this part of the hearing. Sometimes the arbitrator will talk directly and privately with only the parties' representatives.

When all the evidence is in, sometimes the representatives offer closing arguments to the arbitrator. The arbitrator can issue a "bench decision," meaning that the ruling in the case will be made then and there. But more often, each side will submit a written post-hearing brief, and the arbitrator's award will come down in written form some time after the close of the hearing.

Which Cases Go to Arbitration, and Which Don't

By necessity, unions are forced to be quite selective about which cases get processed all the way to arbitration. Depending on the size of the workplace, dozens or hundreds of grievances may be filed each year. Cases that go all the way to arbitration are quite time consuming and can cost the union treasury many thousands of dollars.

In deciding which cases can be taken to arbitration, unions must take into account quite a few factors. Obviously, one prime consideration in choosing whether a particular case can justify the time and expense involved in going to arbitration is how likely it is that the case will come up a winner. All things being equal, a grievance that is likely to be a slam dunk before an arbitrator is a far more likely prospect to be taken that far than a case that is a long shot.

But here, as with everything else in life, all things are not equal. So here are just some of the questions your union must ask in deciding the best way to allocate its limited resources in the grievance/arbitration process.

How Many Are Affected? The outcome of an individual grievance, by definition, directly affects only one person. But a group grievance, or a grievance filed on behalf of the entire bargaining unit, stands to yield a lot more "bang for the buck" if it is successfully pursued to arbitration.

What Is Its Value as a Precedent? Some grievances may be important for a particular individual, but they arise out of unusual occurrences or seldom used provisions of the contract. It is considerably more tempting for a union to go all the way to arbitration in a case where the outcome will likely affect others in the future, such as the first "test case" grievance that arises under important language just negotiated into a contract.

Is There Alternative Relief Available?

In some situations, it may be that an equally effective alternative to a grievance exists. The union may be able to go to a government agency that has enforcement authority or to use political channels to bring pressure to bear, or you and your co-workers may be able to apply some direct pressure on the employer.

What Is the Severity of the Problem?

Terminations—the "capital punishment of the workplace"—understandably will be higher on your union's list of priorities than, say, a warning letter that is placed in an employee's personnel file.

Is This the Right Case to Address the Issue?

Your grievance may address a particular problem, but another grievance might be a better test case: because it has clearer facts or because the employer representative involved handled it less intelligently. So it might make the most sense for the union to take a pass on your case but to go for a victory using another employee's grievance.

What Is the Organizing Potential?

Sometimes pursuing a particular grievance or going all the way to arbitration is part of a larger strategy on the part of the union to address a problem. Perhaps, for example, the publicity surrounding an arbitration case is just one component of the union's plan to raise awareness about a dispute with the employer among those in the workplace or in the community—or to mobilize support for a particular fight.

Keeping the Employer Honest

As you can see, an arbitration proceeding can be quite a time consuming procedure, and it can eat up large chunks of the union treasury. So, all things being equal, it's almost always better if problems can be tackled and resolved right when they arise: the results are quicker and less costly, and you and your co-workers get to enjoy whatever benefits result more quickly.

But it will always be necessary to take at least some grievance cases to arbitration. Sometimes the employer just won't give in at the outset. So if a problem is important enough, the union needs to have the resolve to take the case all the way to a final arbitration decision. Also, it's necessary from time to time to fight a case to the end—and win it—to keep the employer honest the next time a workplace grievance arises.

WHERE DO

workplace rights

COME FROM?

As a union member, your workplace rights come from a number of different sources. Let's take a look at the main kinds of employment protection, so that you can better understand where your rights come from and how you can use your union to protect them.

Just as society has laws that everyone lives by, passed by legislatures, your workplace, too, has its book of statutes: the collective bargaining agreement. We've taken a look at how a union contract is created through the bargaining process, which is very different from the process used to create laws. The end result is the same, however: a collection of the rules that apply to everyone in the workplace, workers and bosses alike, setting forth some things that can be done, other things that must be done, and still others that are totally prohibited. And when someone believes that the rules have been violated, there is the enforcement mechanism of the grievance/arbitration procedure, as we have seen.

Contracts are of varying lengths. Some have a duration of as little as one year, some can go for ten, but most tend to run for several years or so. And sometimes a negotiated Memorandum of Understanding will supplement the contract or some existing contract provisions will be changed in the middle of a contract. No matter how long a contract is in effect, it stands as the law of the workplace.

Beyond the Contract

The collective bargaining agreement negotiated by your union is the key document affecting your worklife. But different workplace rights come from different sources, so it's important to keep in mind what besides the written word of the union contract establishes the set of workplace rights and responsibilities.

Government Laws and Regulations

Many laws apply specifically to workplaces. These may be passed at the federal, state or local level, and some of them result in rather lengthy, detailed regulations. Some—such as wage and hour laws, health and safety statutes, and laws against discrimination—apply to both unionized and non-unionized workplaces. Others come into play only in workplaces where the employees are organizing into a union or already have unionized. The most important laws dealing with workplace rights are discussed later in this chapter.

Employer Handbooks and Regulations

If you work for a company, especially a big one, chances are good that there's a handbook with all sorts of rules on things like attendance, dealing with customers, and other specifics about what's allowed and not allowed on the job. Similarly, the typical government employer has agency regulations that control scheduling of time off, how inclement weather days are determined, and countless other topics. These are areas that may or may not be addressed in the union contract. Though they're not likely to take precedence over specific terms of a contract, they may well be rules that are binding.

Unwritten Laws

Besides what's in the contract, or in the employer's handbook or government regulations, every workplace has its unwritten rules. Just as in everyday life, there are ways of doing things in the workplace that may not be on a page anywhere to read but are accepted by everyone. When you're waiting to get on an elevator, where is it written that you are required to make way for a parent with a toddler? Nowhere, but people understand that that's the way it should be, so that's the way it usually is. Similarly, it may not be written anywhere that it's okay to knock off a little early on Christmas Eve, or that a phone call to check on your children at home is allowed, but that may have developed into the "law of the shop" in your workplace.

Eternal Vigilance Is the Price of Liberty

Don't make the mistake of thinking that the existence of rights on a page somewhere means that you'll always be able to count on those protections. Rights that aren't exercised can in fact disappear over time; you can lose what you don't protect.

So you need to know where your rights come from, and how to use your union to protect them. In practical terms, this means that when your employer breaks the rules, you need to make sure that your union steward knows about it. A steward's job is to be the "eyes and ears" of the union, but a steward can't be everywhere at once, and that's why individual members have the responsibility to be the steward's "eyes and ears." That way, the union/employer structures that are in place can be used to prevent changes for the worse in the day-to-day conditions of the workplace.

Depending on what your collective bargaining agreement says, it may be that the way things are in your workplace—established "past practices"—are actually enforceable under the contract or in another legal forum. Arbitrators resolving contract disputes will sometimes rule that employees have the right to do something the way it's always been done, even if there's no explicit language saying so in the contract.

For example, at night you may park in a close-by customer lot because that's where everyone always parks, even though the contract doesn't say anything about parking. Suppose one day your employer puts up a sign prohibiting parking there. The union may well have a grievance it can win that the "past practice" of parking in that lot can't be changed unilaterally.

Union Constitutions and Bylaws

Your union will also have a constitution and bylaws. These may exist for your local union, your international union or for another intermediate level. Generally, these documents outline the structure of the union, and say how the union is governed. They will, for example, identify the various officers of the union and their authority as well as lay out different election or appointment mechanisms. Procedures dealing with how union meetings are called and how the meetings are conducted will be detailed, as well as what member voting rights are in place for union business such as ratifying a collective bargaining agreement.

The Basic Labor Law Framework

Most people are surprised to learn how many laws are on the books that regulate the workplace lives of workers, both union and non-union.

There are laws at the federal, state and local levels that apply only to you in a unionized environment: laws that govern the right to organize a union, the collective bargaining relationship between an employer and its unionized workforce, and the internal rights and responsibilities of unions and their members. And both you and employees who are not represented by a union are covered by a host of other laws. So in many instances, you as a unionized employee have the best of both worlds: statutory protections provided to all employees, plus the protections your union has been able to negotiate in your particular workplace.

Let's take a look at the overall scheme of labor laws, followed by a brief overview of some of the more important laws covering both unionized and non-unionized workplaces.

The Private Sector

The National Labor Relations Act (NLRA) is the law establishing union rights for most, though not all, employees. The NLRA was passed in 1935 as the Wagner Act, and has been amended since then. Its coverage extends to most employees who do not work for a public employer.

Provisions of the National Labor Relations Act

If you are in the private sector, it was probably under Section 7 of the NLRA that your union exercised its legal right to organize. (If you are a public sector employee, your union rights probably are very similar to those in the NLRA, as we'll discuss shortly.) The act states: "Employees shall have the right to self-organization, to form, join, or assist labor organizations, to bargain collectively through representatives of their own choosing, and to engage in other concerted activities for the purpose of collective bargaining or other mutual aid or protection, and shall also have the right to refrain from any or all such activities . . ."

The National Labor Relations Board, a large federal agency with regional offices in many states, enforces the terms of the act. More likely than not, it was the NLRB that received the union authorization cards signed by you and your co-workers (or those who preceded you in your workplace) and then conducted the union representation election that resulted in your union acquiring formal collective bargaining rights.

Though it functions on an administrative level, the NLRB has a parallel setup to our system of criminal laws. Either because of the words used in the statute itself, or because of regulations or court decisions, certain actions on the part of an employer or a union are defined as unfair labor practices, or ULPs. These ULPs may arise either out of actions that take place in the course of a union organizing drive or after a union already has representation rights. When an unfair labor practice charge is filed, the NLRB first functions as an investigator, gathering evidence from both sides to see whether there is sufficient reason to believe that the law was violated. If the NLRB regional office decides that it does appear that the law was breached, then a formal complaint is issued, and an NLRB attorney serves, in effect, as a prosecutor in the case. A separate branch of the NLRB provides a judge, who conducts a hearing and rules on whether the law was broken.

What are the basic categories of employer conduct that are illegal under the NLRA? Violations of the Section 7 rights include:

♦ statements or actions that interfere with, restrain, or coerce union activity;

♦ domination of unions (that is, any form of a "company union," where the employer really controls the union);

♦ discrimination against employees who engage in union activity;

♦ retaliation against individuals who file unfair labor practice charges or who cooperate with the NLRB in pursuing such charges;

♦ refusal to engage in good faith bargaining with the union.

Keep in mind that, through years of case decisions, these basic rights are given a broader scope than the words themselves might indicate. For example, the right to engage in union activity includes various types of "concerted activity." Suppose the air conditioning system in your workplace keeps breaking down, and it's a hot July. If you and some co-workers gripe to a supervisor about the discomfort, even independent of a formal grievance under your union contract, any retaliation against you by your employer may well be found to violate your rights under the NLRA.

Through a combination of deliberate underfunding by Congress in recent years, anti-worker and anti-union decisions on the part of conservative board appointees and judges, and other factors, the NLRB is not nearly the effective protector of employee and union rights that it should be. Too many cases take far too long to get processed, consuming unions' and employees' limited resources. And the balance between an employer's rights and those of employees and their unions is too often tilted too far in the employer's direction.

As a result of this anti-union, anti-employee enforcement of the national labor law, in recent years unions increasingly have tried to find ways around having to use NLRB procedures. For example, to avoid lengthy delays in election processes, many unions now try to force an employer to recognize the union without petitioning the board for a representation election. Or unions may try to pressure an employer to change its behavior through other means, rather than by filing an unfair labor practice charge. But just the same, the board is often an effective enforcer of union rights, and many a terminated union activist has been reinstated with full back pay, plus interest, as a result of successfully pursuing an unfair labor practice charge.

Limitations . . . and Other Private Sector Labor Law Coverage

The National Labor Relations Act covers only those industries engaged in "interstate commerce." This means that the company in question must conduct at least some business across state lines, and that it must meet a specified "volume of business" standard. As a practical matter, the vast majority of private employers are subject to the provisions of the act.

Even if a particular employer is subject to the provisions of the NLRA, that law still may not include in its coverage certain types of individuals in the workplace. Those who are considered "supervisors," "managers" or "confidential employees" are excluded from the protections of the act. And those classified as "independent contractors," a rapidly growing category in the high-tech industry, have to fight to get themselves covered by the protections of this federal law.

And as outrageous as it might seem, it is the case that two categories of poorly paid and mistreated workers most in need of union rights—agricultural laborers and domestic workers—are not covered by the NLRA or by any other federal labor law granting the right to unionize. But there is *some* good news: undocumented workers are covered by the NLRA's protections.

Adding to the confusing patchwork of labor laws, states sometimes pass their own legislation covering a group of employees excluded from NLRA protections. To its credit, in 1944 Hawaii did so for farmworkers in that state, and in 1975 California did the same.

To make things just a bit more confusing, certain groups of employees in the private sector who are not covered by the NLRA do have union rights under another federal statute. The nation's oldest labor law, the Railway Labor Act, was passed in 1926. As you would guess from its title, this law originally covered those in the railroad industry. But times change, and so does statutory coverage: now, the Railway Labor Act governs most workers in the airline industry as well. If you are covered by this law, be aware that it establishes rules for labor-management relations that differ, sometimes significantly, from those in the NLRA.

The Public Sector — Though the protections of the National Labor Relations Act do not extend to employees outside the private sector, many public sector workers do have statutorily covered union rights.

Federal Employees

Thanks to an executive order issued by President Kennedy in 1962, the substance of which was enacted into law in 1978, most federal employees enjoy the right to unionize. The Federal Labor Relations Authority is the agency that administers the federal sector bargaining law, performing many of the same functions that the NLRB does for private sector employees. The FLRA conducts representation elections to determine if a particular group of federal employees wishes to be represented by a labor union, and it investigates and prosecutes allegations of unfair labor practices. The scope of legal rights granted to federal sector unions is somewhat more restricted than those enjoyed by their private sector counterparts. In particular, the type of subjects that federal sector unions have the right to negotiate with federal agencies is narrower. On the other hand, the consultation rights on a wide range of topics that federal unions enjoy gives them a "foot in the door" that is often quite effective in ensuring that the workers' voice is heard.

State and Local Government Employees

Whether particular public sector employees have union rights is determined by whether a state, county or municipality has chosen to enact such a law.

The first state to do so was Wisconsin, in 1959, following increasingly aggressive union organizing in that state by public sector employees. More than thirty states now have some form of such enabling legislation authorizing unionization by at least some categories of public employees. Many counties and cities similarly provide the right to unionize for some or all of their employees. If you are unionized by virtue of working in one of these jurisdictions, your union and employer operate under a local public sector equivalent of the NLRA. And similar to the legal framework in the federal sector, even for public sector workplaces covered by bargaining legislation, there are always some individuals, such as higher-up managers, who are not eligible for union representation.

Each public sector bargaining law establishes its own definitions for what subjects can be brought up at the bargaining table, what union activities are and are not permitted, and so on. Generally speaking, although a far greater percentage of public sector employees are unionized than their private sector counterparts, public sector unions are more restricted in terms of what they can bargain about, and they are less likely to have the legally protected right to strike.

94

Other Workplace Protection Laws

In addition to the basic laws outlining the right to unionize, more and more often many parts of workplace life are regulated by legislation. Learning the exact coverage of these laws can be a pretty complex undertaking, depending on whether you are in the public sector or private sector, working in a particular industry, employed by a large or small company, and many other factors. We won't try to specify an exact listing of which laws apply to you. Rather, here's an idea of what worker protection laws generally cover; consult with your union representatives or a lawyer if you spot what may be a violation of your rights. Remember, too, that in many instances, you as a union-represented worker enjoy the best of both worlds: the statutory protections of a particular law, plus your union contract rights.

Here is a quick rundown of the range of subjects covered by workplace legislation and the types of protections such laws contain.

Wages and Hours

The Fair Labor Standards Act (FLSA) is the federal law setting the minimum wage and standards for overtime pay. Administered by the Department of

Labor, this law is far-reaching. Keep in mind, though, that when a state or local law—or, of course, your union contract—sets more favorable standards, those will govern. Workplaces must display a poster informing you of your FLSA statutory rights.

The minimum wage set by federal law is only a fraction of the amount that, according to the government's own calculations, is needed to live above the poverty level. (That's why in dozens of jurisdictions around the country, labor-community coalitions already have succeeded in requiring that, at the local level, a "living wage" must be paid by companies that receive local government contracts, subsidies or tax breaks.)

The FLSA also requires payment at one and one-half times your regular rate of pay for all hours worked beyond forty in a workweek. This law doesn't set any maximum number of hours that can be worked in a day or a week, though, or regulate holiday pay, shift differentials, or anything like that. Any such restrictions or entitlements—and the special pay provisions attached to them—will be found in your union contract.

Already weak, the FLSA goes on to exempt a number of types of employees from its minimum wage and/or overtime requirements. Those who are categorized as executive, administrative or professional employees—broad groups that include teachers in elementary and secondary schools, outside sales employees, and some skilled computer professionals—are not covered by the minimum wage or the overtime pay requirements. Other types of employees—including farmworkers and live-in domestic service workers—are excluded completely from the overtime pay requirements. In addition, special rules apply for workers who ordinarily earn tips from customers. These rules cover both the direct wages that must be paid and how the amount in monthly tips calculates into wages.

Discrimination: Equal Employment Opportunity Commission (EEOC)

Many federal, state and local laws outlaw a number of different kinds of discrimination against both job applicants and current employees. The broadest federal law, known as Title VII of the Civil Rights Act of 1964, prohibits discrimination based on an employee's race, color, religion, sex, or national origin. Its coverage extends to most private sector employees, plus federal, state and local government workers.

Unlawful discrimination can come up in any aspect of your compensation or conditions of employment: pay determinations, hiring or firing decisions, promotion or transfer opportunities, or job training and apprenticeship programs. Illegal sex discrimination includes sexual harassment, and the protections of federal law extend to certain forms of discrimination against pregnant women. For example, a federal law called the Pregnancy Discrimination Act says that your employer can't place any restrictions on use of maternity leave (covering pregnancy, childbirth, and related medical conditions) that aren't also imposed on other uses of disability or sick leave. These federal laws are administered by the Equal Employment Opportunity Commission (EEOC), a federal government agency with the power to investigate and bring enforcement actions against an employer.

The EEOC also oversees a 1990 federal law, the Americans with Disabilities Act. This law prohibits discrimination based on an employee's disability, and it requires employers to make reasonable workplace accommodations for a qualified employee with a disability. A counterpart statute, the Rehabilitation Act of 1973, provides very similar protections for federal employees and for those working for government contractors.

A third federal law, the Equal Pay Act of 1963, is enforced by the EEOC. This law requires that women and men receive the same pay for doing "substantially similar" work. This means equal pay for the same type of job. This law does not address the big problem of "comparable worth"—when women are paid less than men for doing different jobs, but jobs requiring a comparable level of skill and experience. A particular employer may have a higher pay rate for (mostly male) plumbers than for (mostly female) secretaries, even though the two jobs require roughly similar levels of education, degrees of skill and experience, and so on.

Finally, the EEOC enforces the terms of the Age Discrimination in Employment Act of 1967 (ADEA). This law provides protection against discrimination for those who are forty years of age or older.

Discrimination: Other Laws

Almost every state has its own civil rights law, giving protection to employees—public and private sector—who work in that state. Countless state, county and municipal laws and ordinances add other categories of individuals protected from discriminatory actions. This means that even though the federal laws mentioned above don't bar discrimination based on such factors as sexual orientation, marital or parental status, or arrest and conviction records, you may be protected by another law that does.

Business Closings

The 1989 federal Worker Adjustment and Retraining Notification Act (WARN) applies to most businesses with 100 or more employees, requiring that they give sixty days' advance notice before closing a facility or conducting a mass layoff. This law is supposed to give workers and their families some transition time to adjust to the loss of employment, including obtaining retraining to make it easier to find a new job.

Your union contract probably has provisions that will come into play if there's a shutdown or layoff. These contractual rights go far beyond what the law provides for employees who don't have a union—another instance where being represented gives you two layers of protection.

The WARN law won't stop a company from making business decisions based on its economic condition. But this law is still a valuable one. As a practical matter, the sixty-day "heads up" to a union can provide the time needed to organize community opposition to the company's decision or to apply some other form of pressure to turn it around.

Family and Medical Leave

As a first step—though not a very big one—in 1993 the Family and Medical Leave Act (FMLA) went into effect, intended to provide a means for employees to balance their work and family responsibilities. It does this by saying that workers are legally entitled to take unpaid leave because of any of the following: the birth, care, or adoption or foster care of a child; the care of an immediate family member with a serious health condition; or the employee's own serious health condition. This law also gives returning employees the right to go back to their old jobs, or to equivalent positions, without being penalized. The Department of Labor can investigate FMLA claims and enforce the terms of the law. Because the FMLA doesn't cover all workplaces and requires an employer to grant only unpaid leave (and then only under certain circumstances), your union contract will likely contain better provisions. And if this is the case, the rights in your union contract will have priority over those in this federal law.

The Rights of Veterans and Reservists

Veterans and reservists who served on active duty for at least 180 days and who did not receive a dishonorable discharge, or were released or discharged from active duty because of a service-connected disability, are covered by federal laws providing for job counseling, training, and placement services, as well as re-employment by their preservice employer. In some cases, the law entitles them to preferential treatment in getting a job.

Employees of government contractors who have a service-connected disability have legal protections against certain types of employment discrimination. The Department of Labor investigates claims under these laws and has the authority to take appropriate enforcement action.

Health and Safety

There is a confusing patchwork of laws and agencies that govern workplace health and safety matters, but they're all extremely important. Six thousand American workers are killed on the job each year, and there are far too many instances of unnecessary workplace injuries and illnesses. The best-known workplace health and safety law is OSHA, the Occupational Safety and Health Act, which is administered by the Department of Labor's Occupational Safety and Health Administration, also called OSHA. Some workplaces (such as those in the coal mining industry) are regulated by a separate law, and almost half the states administer their own, federally approved programs for public sector employees. Other laws and federal agencies, such as the Environmental Protection Agency, play a role as well. And in all likelihood, your union contract has extra protections for your workplace health and safety.

There are a lot of different sources of rights and responsibilities in this area, but the general standards and principles apply pretty much across the board, covering such things as temperature, air quality, lighting and cleanliness in the workplace, exposure to hazardous substances and radiation, and being provided with necessary personal protective equipment, such as respirators, safety goggles and the like.

The federal OSHA law says that employers have a "general duty" to provide work and a workplace free from recognized hazards that are "likely to cause death or serious physical harm." Not surprisingly, unions and employers have a lot of differences about the specifics of what's safe and what isn't. OSHA has set specific standards on some particular workplace hazards—exposure to asbestos, for example, or rules for working around certain kinds of machinery—and organized labor is fighting for many more.

As with the Fair Labor Standards Act, workplaces covered by OSHA are required by law to display in a visible place the official OSHA poster that describes everyone's rights and responsibilities under the law. Your steward should be able to answer any questions you may have or to get the needed information from someone more knowledgeable. In fact, your union contract may well have established a union health and safety committee, which means that there is already in place a knowledgeable group of individuals to deal with your health and safety concerns. While it's almost always best to work through your union, individuals have the right to contact OSHA or whatever agency administers your workplace health and safety law to get specific answers about your rights or to file a formal complaint requesting an inspection— usually conducted with no advance notice—of hazardous conditions. (If you do request a workplace inspection, it is possible to have your name withheld from your employer.)

In addition to standards for a workplace free of safety and health hazards, you and your union also have the right to information. Your employer is required to maintain, and to keep available for inspection, certain types of documents. The agencies that administer the law also must furnish you with certain information. Workplace health and safety documents that can be obtained include:

◆ the Log and Summary of Occupational Injuries, known as OSHA Form 200. This contains information on the number of safety and illness incidents at your workplace and time lost due to them. Your employer is required to produce these records for review for the past five years.

◆ copies of the standards, rules, regulations, and requirements that apply to your workplace, including the OSH Act itself.

◆ information on hazardous chemicals as well as relevant employee exposure and medical records, plus information as to what measures the employer is taking to reduce improper exposure levels.

While you need to be very careful in taking this step, under certain conditions, you and your co-workers may also have the right, under the Occupational Safety and Health Act and the National Labor Relations Act, to refuse to do unsafe work. To have legal protection for this, the law says that you must have a reasonable belief that there is an imminent danger of death or serious injury, with the risk being great enough so as to make it impractical to first request an inspection by OSHA or take some other, less drastic step. You will strengthen the legal protection available to you if you are in a position to notify your supervisor before stopping work, and also alert the union and your co-workers beforehand, to enlist their support for collective action. You're best off if you don't refuse the assignment outright; instead, say that you will do the job, once it is made safe.

Finally, there is protection under the law against any reprisal against you if you exercise any of your rights, such as requesting a workplace inspection or access to relevant records, or even just complaining to your employer.

Whistleblowing

A "whistleblower" is an employee who gives information to the public, the news media, or a government agency about some employer activity that is illegal or improper. Because the disclosure of information about corruption, cost overruns, or production of defective or harmful products can seriously damage an employer, you often see retaliation against whistleblowers.

But the U.S. Constitution and many federal, state and local laws provide protection for at least some people who blow the whistle. Since the stakes are often high, be very cautious if you are thinking of "going public" with sensitive information. Don't go around chatting with those who don't have a "need to know"; consult in confidence with a union officer or with an attorney of your choosing for expert guidance on the best and safest way to get out the information you have.

ERISA: Federal Pension Law

Laws—written, not coincidentally, by lawyers—can be pretty fearsome and complicated creatures. But the law that governs virtually all private employer—provided pension and retirement benefit plans, known as ERISA, probably wins the prize for "Most Difficult to Understand by a Normal Human Being." When it was passed, ERISA quickly gained the sarcastic nickname "The Full Employment Act for Lawyers."

What's easy to understand is that ERISA provides two important types of protections. There are substantive rights, such as requirements for when an employee must be able to vest (that is, how many years must be worked before being eligible for a pension) in what are known as "defined benefit" plans. (These are the older types of pension plans, where the dollar amount of your eventual pension payments is based on your years of employment and earnings, as opposed to "defined contribution" plans, where the employer makes contributions to an individual IRA-type fund for you.) ERISA also contains many procedural protections for employees—for example, requiring that a claims procedure for benefits be in place and that a great deal of information about the plan and your coverage be made available.

Immigration Laws

Labor unions, immigrant advocacy groups, and employers have fought for years over what federal law should say about employers hiring workers who are not U.S. citizens. The battle is an important one because of how such laws can encourage tensions and conflicts among workers based on their nationality or how they can stand in the way of discriminatory employment decisions based on national origin.

To control the hiring of undocumented workers, federal law—and possibly your union contract—sets forth requirements as to what personal identification documents your employer can insist upon seeing, and when.

101

Workers' Compensation

Almost all American workers are now covered by workers' compensation. This is an automatic type of insurance program, based on a no-fault concept: if you are injured or disabled in connection with your job, you receive a set payment for your loss and reimbursement for any medical expenses, and you are eligible for weekly disability payments.

Workers' compensation is a mixed blessing for workers. On the one hand, the uniform laws and set schedules for payment increase the chances of getting mandatory compensation for your loss, and can cut down on the need for time-consuming and expensive litigation. On the other hand, these laws take away your right to sue your employer for negligence and to recover damages for pain and suffering. This means that you may not end up receiving the amount of compensation that you deserve.

Time limits are extremely important in pursuing some of your rights under workers' compensation laws, so consult with your union steward immediately if you're hurt on the job. When in doubt about whether your injury is work-related, ask questions: you may learn, for example, that even some injuries that occur during your commute to or from work may be covered by the law.

IF YOU GET IN

trouble . . .

W hether you're "innocent" or "guilty," one day you may find yourself called into your supervisor's office to answer questions. The grilling may be about an alleged problem with your job performance. Or it may be about serious misconduct, like an accusation that you've stolen property from work or cheated on a timesheet.

Your first thought may be "I haven't done anything wrong" or "I haven't done anything different than what folks do around here all the time, so there's no harm in answering a few questions." But many workers (like many criminal defendants) find themselves in hot water when an over-eager supervisor or company investigator deliberately twists perfectly innocent answers to questions or takes answers out of context to create a misleading impression. So better safe than sorry; educate yourself now about your basic rights in this area, so you can use them if you have to.

Unfortunately, in the workplace we don't have all the rights that we saw growing up when we watched someone in a movie or on TV getting questioned by the police. There's no workplace equivalent of the *Miranda* right to remain silent, or even notification of the right to have a lawyer (or union steward, in your case) present. If you're asked questions about a work-related matter, you do have to give answers.

But you can—and should—provide yourself with the protection you will have if a union representative is present:

♦ your steward can learn beforehand what the questioning is going to be about;

♦ you can consult with your steward privately before the questioning starts;

♦ your steward can keep a written record of the meeting and serve as a witness afterward about what you said; and

♦ your steward can make sure the questioning stays within reasonable bounds.

Your rights to union representation are known as "*Weingarten* rights," after a 1975 U.S. Supreme Court ruling. At first these rights applied only to private sector employees covered by the National Labor Relations Act. But through legislation and subsequent court decisions these basic protections are now generally extended to federal employees, as well as to many state and local government workers.

Under *Weingarten* you have the legal right to have a union representative (but not a lawyer) present during a meeting with management if *all* of the following conditions are met:

1. The meeting is an investigatory interview. This means that you are expected to answer questions in connection with an inquiry into possible wrongdoing or unacceptable behavior. *Weingarten* rights do not cover meetings where the communication is one-way; that is, when the purpose is merely to convey information to you or to notify you of a decision already made regarding discipline.

2. Disciplinary action *may* result from the meeting. The law requires only that disciplinary action—of any severity—is one possible result of the meeting.

3. You "reasonably believe" that disciplinary action may result. If there is a

legal dispute over whether your concern about possible disciplinary action is "reasonable," the determination will be made based on all the circumstances surrounding the meeting: Has your supervisor previously raised the possibility of discipline? Have other employees already been disciplined for what you're accused of? Are you already working under the threat of a performance warning letter?

4. You make a request for representation. This is another way *Weingarten* rights differ from *Miranda* rights: your employer generally is under no obligation to inform you of your right to be represented. It's up to you to know your rights, and to assert them.

So here's some practical advice if a supervisor wants to ask you questions about something on the job:

◆ Ask what the meeting will be about. If the answer confirms that the employer is indeed looking into something of a disciplinary nature, then insist on having a union representative present. You should say something along the following lines: "Since it seems to me that this meeting might lead to a disciplinary action being taken against me, I request that my union representative be present. If you will not allow this, I will respectfully decline to answer any questions unless you order me to do so." If it's not clear at first whether you might end up being disciplined, ask if there is "any possibility" that disciplinary action may result. If you get any answer besides "no," then insist on having a union representative present before going any further. (If someone isn't available then and there, ask for the meeting to be rescheduled for a time when a representative can be there.)

◆ If your request for representation is denied, think twice before you refuse to answer questions. It's risky to do that, since you then face the possibility of being disciplined for not answering work-related questions. Instead, it's usually wiser to make it clear that you will answer questions only if you are directed to do so. After proceeding under protest, you can consult your union steward about the best way to challenge the denial of representation.

105

Protection from Retaliation

It's easy enough for legislators to pass laws establishing workplace rights. And it's easy for you to read about them in this book. But everybody knows that in the Real World, it sometimes takes more than a little guts to exercise your rights. Everyone has seen examples, in the workplace and outside of it, where an individual speaking up then has to deal with the consequences of having made someone in a position of power unhappy.

If you are faced with making a decision about whether to assert your rights, or to just go on with things the way they are, there are few important considerations to keep in mind.

First, there are many legal protections available to those who speak up and invoke their rights. Section 7 of the National Labor Relations Act (see pages 90–92) provides legal protection against retaliation for those who speak or act with their co-workers to deal with their working conditions. Any retaliation by your employer can be challenged by filing an unfair labor practice charge with the National Labor Relations Board. (Laws governing labor relations for federal and other public employees also contain these protections.)

And remember that most of the laws discussed in this and the preceding chapter have their own provisions that make it illegal for your employer to retaliate against you in any way for exercising rights under that particular statute, including protection if you file a charge or complaint. Suppose, for example, you pursue a discrimination action, alleging that you were denied a promotion based on your race. After you've filed the charge, you find yourself moved to a lousy shift in a sister location seventy-five miles from your home. It may turn out in the end that you don't have enough proof to overturn the decision to deny you the promotion, but you may be able to get your shift and work location restored because that employer action will be found to be retaliation for your having filed the initial charge.

Risky, But Worth It

Be aware that there sometimes is a difference between what you know actually occurred and what you can prove as a matter of law. You'd be kidding yourself if you thought that there's never been an instance in which a worker was in fact retaliated against for having engaged in behavior that is legally protected but was unable to prove that the retaliation took place. Still, don't let this prevent you from asserting your rights. There have been plenty more instances where the agency charged with enforcing a law moved aggressively against an employer trying to prevent an employee from asserting rights under that law. After all, if all employees are successfully intimidated into not using the provisions of the law, that agency becomes useless. (And again, remember your double layer of union protection: reprisals can be defended against through the grievance/arbitration procedure in a good number of union contracts.)

Also remember that, just as in all other aspects of life, there can be no forward progress without some degree of risk taking. True, you may be opening yourself up to some new problems on the job if you take action against existing problems. But if you do nothing, the two most likely outcomes are (1) the current problems will remain or (2) the current problems will just get worse.

THE

union's face

OUTSIDE THE WORKPLACE

We've taken a look at how your union is set up and how it functions inside the workplace. But to paint a more complete picture of what unions are and what they do, let's turn to the broader labor union agenda in two critical areas: organizing and politics.

The Need to Organize

At different points in the history of American unions, organizing activity has taken place at varying levels of intensity. Depending on how aggressively unions were organizing, and because of changes elsewhere in society, the total percentage of union membership has changed dramatically over the years. Organizing among some types of employees—notably government workers—has been steadily increasing for many years now. Thanks partly to a significantly higher victory rate in public sector union elections than in those in the private sector, well over one third of organized labor now consists of government employees. But despite the vigorous growth of public sector union organizing, overall the percentage of the American workforce that is unionized underwent a steady, decades-long decline as the twenty-first century approached.

Working in a unionized workplace, you may think that it doesn't make much of a difference to you how much new union organizing is going on elsewhere. You may even be uncomfortable with the fact that part of your hard-earned dues dollars are devoted to winning union protection for others, rather than being spent on negotiations and representation in your own workplace. But there are good reasons why supporting union efforts to organize the unorganized makes sense—not just for other workers who need help, but for you, too.

Immediate Gain

Every day, in some direct or indirect way, you experience the benefits of unionization. Today may or may not be the day that the discipline provision in your contract saves your job, or that union enforcement of health and safety standards prevents you from being injured, or that you are able to get the day off—with pay—to care for your sick child. But even if something this apparent does not take place, for almost all workers today is the day that you earn more money than you would have without a union—and have better health coverage and other benefits. Many statistical studies have documented the dollars-and-cents difference that union membership contributes to. In 1999, for example, according to the U.S. Department of Labor: unionized workers on average earned 30 percent more than non-union workers; unionized women earned 35 percent more than non-union women; unionized Latinos earned 35 percent more than non-union Latinos; and unionized African-Americans earned 39 percent more than non-union African-Americans. There's no question that your quality of life is better because you are union-represented. And it's the right thing to do to help others gain that same level of protection. We make society better for all when each of us makes a personal decision to pitch in and help others acquire what we already have.

Protecting What We've Won

Even if what you are most focused on is conditions in your own workplace, here's something to consider: successful union organizing in other workplaces will improve things for you.

How much clout your union has at the bargaining table and in the legislative arena and elsewhere often is determined by "union density." This term refers to the degree to which employees in your particular industry or geographic area are unionized. Simply stated, the greater the percentage of employees who are unionized, the more power each union has to win and enforce good contracts and to be an influential part of the process to enact a labor-friendly legislative agenda. Many statistical studies have shown that unions are better able to negotiate higher wages for the employees they represent when the employees of employers in the same competitive market are organized.

One interesting illustration of how union density can translate into dollars and cents in the paycheck is what happened in the automobile industry over the last couple of decades of the twentieth century. From 1978 to 1997, union membership in the segment of the auto industry that produces parts for the Big Three automakers declined from 24 percent to 10 percent. Back when 24 percent of the workers making electrical parts for engines were represented by the United Auto Workers, the average parts worker earned 93 percent of the wages paid by the Big Three automakers. Almost 20 years later, when union membership for those making electrical parts had declined to 10 percent, that average wage had dropped to only 63 percent of what a Big Three worker earned. What's the lesson here? Well, if you were a UAW member in the parts industry, you suffered financially, in part because an increasing percentage of your co-workers elsewhere were not organized. But there's another lesson, too: most labor economists will tell you that this decrease in union density also hurt unionized workers at the Big Three. Having the wage floor set by non-unionized workers drop lower and lower made it harder for the UAW to resist downward pressures on their Big Three members' earnings when they went to the bargaining table.

Many such examples, all over the country, led the 1995 Economic Report of the President to conclude that a "significant portion of the increase in wage inequality during the last fifteen years" was due to the decline in unionization. (And if anyone tells you that the reason American workers' earnings have gone down is that we just don't work hard enough, point out that this decline in wages took place at the same time that American worker productivity was rising.)

Helping Other Workers

Almost all current union members were hired into an already represented workplace. But while you personally may have played no role in unionizing your place of work, you can't assume that those who did had an easy time of it. In the early decades of union organizing in the United States, it was not unusual for employers to respond to union organizing drives with

111

physical violence. Many of the early industrial unions got their footholds only by standing up to a court system that jailed union supporters, and to the clubs and guns of company thugs. Sometimes the bullets that maimed and killed union supporters and their families were fired by state militias or federal troops, serving as private armies for anti-union employers.

In the decades since, we've moved on to considerably "kinder, gentler" forms of resistance to union organizing drives, particularly in the public sector. But even if your workplace was organized in the post–World War II era, it is quite likely that your predecessors had to stand up to significant attempts by your employer to intimidate union supporters. While those who came before you may not have had to dodge company bullets, they did have to maintain the courage of their convictions to stand together in the face of modern-day employer responses to organizing drives that include:

112

♦ illegal threats to shut down if the workplace is organized—a threat that is made in more than half of recent union organizing drives;

♦ illegally firing employees who decide to become actively involved in organizing drives—something that takes place in more than one third of all organizing drives;

♦ using outside consultants to mastermind anti-union campaigns, including surveillance and intimidation tactics that skirt and violate the law—a tactic of 80 percent of employers; and

♦ holding "captive audience" meetings, where employees are forced to listen to carefully packaged anti-union propaganda—a device used by over 90 percent of employers.

And once the union comes in, one battle may be over but the war is far from won. In about one third of newly organized workplaces, using stall and delay tactics, the employer succeeds in preventing the union from ever winning a first contract.

So you've not only got a legacy to protect in keeping the union strong in your workplace, but you also have good reason to lend a hand to your unorganized fellow workers who may be facing significant obstacles to their

PAYING THE PRICE—IN BLOOD

Organizers and activists face considerable pressure these days to abandon their efforts to band together in their unions. But for victories in worker organizing in the early years, there was often a price paid in blood.

In 1914, members of the United Mine Workers of America in Ludlow, Colorado, went out on strike against a company that was part of the Rockefeller industrial empire. As was routine in those days, the company promptly evicted the miners and their families from the company-owned housing. So the mining families set up a tent colony, which then was surrounded by the National Guard.

As the strike wore on, sometimes at night the militia would shoot their rifles into the colony. For greater protection, the miners dug a cave inside the largest tent, where they moved their family members who were among them.

On Easter night, while the miners and their families were asleep, company thugs and members of the National Guard poured oil on the strikers' tents and set the tents ablaze. As the men, women, and children ran from the inferno, they were machine-gunned.

The death toll—the price paid for seeking a better life through a union—was over a dozen of the children and wives of the miners. Strikers were placed on a blacklist, preventing them from holding jobs in the coal industry.

And how did the courts deal with what became known as the Ludlow Massacre? Scores of the miners and their union leaders were placed under arrest. Of Rockefeller and the other owners, the detective agency brought in to suppress the strike, and the state militia who fired into the tents, not a single one was brought to justice.

But although the Ludlow strikers didn't get their union recognized, the story didn't end there. Fellow mine workers and members of other unions in Colorado attacked scabs at other mines. Rockefeller himself was hounded, including by a minister who protested in front of a New York church that Rockefeller attended. (The minister was beaten by police.) It took some time, and more deaths, but the United Mine Workers succeeded in establishing a strong union presence in the western mine industry.

113

THE UNION MEMBER'S COMPLETE GUIDE

efforts to unionize.

Your Role in Organizing

If you're persuaded about the importance of your union's external organizing efforts, you probably are glad that you're making a financial contribution toward that effort (through part of union dues, or perhaps a special assessment for an organizing fund). But you're not off the hook just yet: as with many other areas of the day-to-day work of the union, it's not enough to pay your money and let the union take care of doing the work.

There are two reasons for you to become personally involved in organizing activity outside of your workplace. First, a healthy, effective union is one in which the members pitch in to do the work, greatly increasing the people-resources of the union. Second, no matter how skilled professional union staff may be—if there is one at all—there is an extra measure of credibility when an already-organized employee speaks directly to an unorganized worker about day-to-day experiences. The successes of member-to-member organizing are clear: one study issued by the AFL-CIO, for example, documents that unions win representation elections in 73 percent of the organizing drives conducted by ordinary members but in only 17 percent of those conducted by professional staff.

The Importance of Politics

Just as with corporations, there are legal limitations on the right of the union to make financial contributions in an election. For that reason, your union may have a political action committee, or PAC, funded with nondues dollars voluntarily contributed by members. And certainly at the local level or above, your union is likely to be involved in trying to influence the workings of mayors, governors and other elected officials, and of legislatures and other political bodies. If unions don't lobby for workplace health and safety laws, for example, or for a higher minimum wage, then who will?

Over the years, most unions have learned that if they try to compete for political influence with business on a dollar-for-dollar basis, the union comes up short. Those pursuing businesses' political interests simply have far more money than workers and our allies do. In fact, the imbalance in money contributed to candidates and parties by business as opposed to the amount contributed by unions ran eleven to one in the 2000 national elections.

**Elect the
Boss**

Why should you care about your union's involvement in the world of politics? As is the case with external organizing, what your union does on the political landscape has a very direct impact on your union's effectiveness in your and other workplaces. Perhaps the most dramatic example of the direct connection between the political arena and the world of collective bargaining is the situation in which public employees find themselves. It is not an oversimplification to say that public employees get to elect the boss when they get involved in electoral campaigns and in how politicians subsequently carry out their duties. It would be throwing away a critical source of leverage if a public employee union did not strive to have influence over the elected government officials who directly determine how much money is budgeted for union members' salaries and benefits.

**Influence Inside
and Outside the
Workplace**

And for every employee, both those in the public sector and those in the private sector, what goes on in the world of politics has a direct connection to the union's ability to advance and protect the members' interests. Legislatures pass and enforce laws that can make it easier or harder for unions to organize, to protect members' health and safety, to bargain for reasonable health care coverage, and to improve countless other aspects of working life. What is won at a bargaining table can be taken away with a stroke of a pen by elected officials who are not worker-friendly, or by appointed or elected judges.

115

On an even broader scale, the priorities that are set by our elected leaders determine in large part what resources will be available to us, as organized workers. To take one example, in 1994 for the first time the California Department of Corrections budget rose higher than that for the University of California. It's not just a question of what effect this had on unionized employees at the University of California. Think about this: when our society decides to spend more on prisons than on schools, what are the prospects for those of us who would like to be able to send our kids to get a good college education, with tuition that is affordable? And no matter how well our unions can negotiate at the bargaining table, what kind of society are we living in if we allow the political choice to be made that two thirds of the inmates in our nation's prisons will be African-American or Hispanic?

your role

IN YOUR UNION

In any society, each individual has to make a fundamental decision about how to relate to the larger group. Some choose not to take very seriously at all the degree to which their participation in group decision making and action can make a difference. These people don't educate themselves as to what is going on. They don't read a daily newspaper or watch the TV news, they don't bother to vote in elections, and they don't join the PTA or get very involved in their kids' schooling. What such folks often do spend a lot of time doing is complaining about the decisions that elected government officials make, the quality of public education, and lots of other things that they have chosen not to become involved in.

There is another approach, of course, to involvement in society. Most of us realize that the more we as individuals educate ourselves as to what is going on around us, and the more we actively participate in shaping the future, the better off everyone is. This is not to say that our society is a perfectly functioning democracy. A lot of policies are set and actions carried out based more on who has the money or power than on what the majority of people really think. But the more that individuals choose to opt out of the decisions that are made, the less democratic things become, and the less our society reflects what most people really want.

The decision you have to make, as an individual represented by a union, is really no different. You can choose not to keep informed about union issues and the actions taken by the union, and not to participate in the daily life of the union. Then, just as with what happens in the larger society, you can gripe about who's running the union and the lousy decisions they make. But there is an alternative, of course: since your union is nothing more than a collection of individual members, you can choose to become involved, and in so doing shape what your union is and what it does.

So if you want to "own" your union, and to share in the members' responsibility of running it, what can you do?

Educate Yourself

If you're going to participate in the union decisions that affect your workplace life, you should do so intelligently. This means taking the time to learn about the union and the issues it is dealing with on behalf of the members. If you don't have a copy of the union contract, get one and look through it, at least enough to get a good idea about what topics are covered and what the specifics are. Make a mental note not only of what rights the union is already in a position to protect but also what improvements you'd like to see in the next round of bargaining.

Your union probably puts out one or more newsletters, magazines, or newspapers designed to fill members in on the issues of the day. And these days, national unions and lots of locals have websites with information about union activities and issues. Treat these like your daily newspaper or weekly news magazine: you certainly don't have to read every word, but devoting a little bit of time can yield a lot of useful information. Most unions also have publications on specific topics, such as explaining your health and safety rights, the union's political action program, and so on. Find out from your steward what's available, and learn what you need to know.

Your union holds periodic meetings open to all members, as well as business meetings of leadership bodies that you can attend as an observer. At the local, regional, or national level, there may be workshops or training programs that you can attend to learn about specific topics. Often, these programs are presented at no or minimal cost to interested members.

If you're going to participate in the workings of your union, it's probably not a bad idea to check out the union's constitution and bylaws. These documents will specify when and how union meetings and elections are conducted, what committees and other structures the union uses to do its work, and what rights members have to participate in such matters as contract ratification votes.

In the process of trying to learn more about your union and what it does, you will undoubtedly have lots of questions. Your union steward is a Jack or Jane of All Trades, with a job description that's pretty lengthy, but first on the list is helping members understand the union's actions. So don't hesitate to insist on answers that will make you a better informed "union citizen."

Be a Set of "Eyes and Ears"

The first instruction given to new union stewards is that they need to be the "eyes and ears" of the union in the workplace. A union contract isn't worth the paper it's printed on if its terms aren't enforced by the union when the employer is in violation. But "the union" can't take any action unless it knows what the facts are, so union stewards serve as fact gatherers who can report what's going on to others with responsibility for putting together the right responses.

119

Union stewards can't be everywhere at once, and they can't see or hear personally everything that goes on the workplace. So part of your job as an individual union member is to be on the lookout for things that the union needs to know about, and to pass along the necessary information. If, for example, a change is made in working conditions but too long a period of time passes before a grievance is filed, it may be too late to challenge the employer's unilateral action. So it's part of your responsibility as an individual union member to be the union's "eyes and ears" in your workplace.

Show Solidarity

It's pretty easy to understand in the abstract the notion that "an injury to one is an injury to all." And it's also not too complicated to grasp that if I don't speak up when someone else is being mistreated, that person isn't likely to be there for me when I need some support.

But what's needed, of course, is for each of us to "walk the walk" and not just "talk the talk." So if your co-workers on the night shift are getting cheated out of their differential, the test is whether you and your co-workers on the day shift make it your business to make sure that the union can do what's needed to take on the employer.

And solidarity extends outside of the workplace, too. If your union—or another union—needs some bodies on a picket line or some other visible expression of support for a fight at another workplace, you need to pitch in. Sometimes the favor will get returned in a very direct way, when your picket line tomorrow is joined by strikers you backed up yesterday. But even without such a one-to-one tradeoff, it's clear that building the overall union movement strengthens your union's rights in your workplace as well.

Be a Union Emissary

One of your union steward's responsibilities is to greet new employees and fill them in on the union. But you can supplement this function very effectively by making a point of talking to newly hired workers about your personal experiences with the union, and making sure that they sign up. Having the union talked up by someone who is not a union official of any kind can go a long way toward creating the needed state of mind that when you get right down to it, the union is "us," not some separate organization.

Your role as a union ambassador is perhaps even more critical outside the workplace. There are a lot of popular misconceptions about what unions are and what they do. You don't have to look far to find people buying into stereotypes that portray unions as consisting of nothing but fat cat bureaucrats living the good life off of hard-earned dues dollars and cutting shady deals with employers and politicians.

Though stereotypes can contain a grain of truth, this negative image is not at all an accurate depiction of the reality of labor unions today. Why is the public perception of the labor union movement so at odds with the day-to-day reality? A large part of the explanation is that the vast majority of Americans are not represented by a labor union, and many Americans have never had any direct experience at all in a unionized workplace. With little firsthand knowledge to go on, some people easily buy into the employers' twisted version of things.

To increase public support for unions and the causes that we fight for inside and out of the workplace, it's important for people to have an accurate view of the role that unions play. And this is where you come in: if you make a point of letting friends and neighbors know about your own experiences as a unionized employee, this can be the most effective way possible to correct popular distortions about the labor movement. To get an accurate picture of what a real-life union is all about, people need to hear firsthand from a real-life unon member.

Sometimes the most effective way to educate others as to the realities of unions is to enlist their support directly in a union fight at your or another workplace. Think about asking members of community or religious groups you are involved in, or your neighbors or others, to sign a petition, show up on a picket line, or make phone calls in support of a union effort in your community or elsewhere. The act of trying to persuade others to take such action may be the most direct way to get the dialogue going that will educate them as to the important role that unions play in society.

Get Involved

Part of the work that unions do is accomplished, at least in larger unions, by paid union staff members, who earn their living conducting arbitration hearings, bargaining contracts, signing up members, and doing all of the other jobs that make a union effective. And some tasks are taken care of by stewards and union officers, who may get some time off or some additional compensation to do their union work.

But the resources of any union are limited, and there is always much more that unions could do to be even more effective in defending the members' interests. A union's power is unleashed when individual members take it upon themselves to pitch in and each does a little something to contribute to the larger effort. No matter what kind of person you are, you have something you can contribute to make your union stronger. If you have good writing skills, you might volunteer to work on the local newsletter. If you have some expertise in health care benefits or health and safety matters, you might volunteer to serve on a committee or help out during contract negotiations. At the very least, we've all got at least a little time to spare once or twice a month, so why not volunteer to help hand-deliver union literature to your fellow employees?

Work for Change

In the larger society in which we live, sometimes things aren't working well at all, and quite a bit of effort is needed to turn things around. Citizens sometimes have to organize among themselves, going door-to-door to enlist the support of others in the community, to "throw out the bums" at election time, or to straighten out a nonresponsive school board or another group making decisions that affect us.

You may be in a similar situation in your workplace life. You may have had the feeling reading parts of this book that the descriptions of how unions work on behalf of their members to improve working conditions don't fully match up to the reality that you have experienced. But just as in the larger society, the solution is not simply to give up; unions, like societies, ultimately are democratic, and change for the better is always possible.

So if your situation is that all is not well within your union, what are the steps that you need to take? First, educate yourself as to how the union is supposed to work. The information discussed earlier on union constitutions and bylaws, and the various laws that govern union activities, should give you a good starting point for understanding what your union ought to be doing, and your rights to have a say.

Second, the key to success always lies in collective action. If you are dissatisfied with how your union goes about its business, then others must be, as well. Find co-workers who want to bring about change, and figure out together what can be done. Sometimes, the solution is no more difficult than communicating with the proper individuals in positions of responsibility in the union; make sure that they understand why you're dissatisfied and the efforts you're willing to undertake to improve things. Other times, of course, you will encounter a great deal more resistance. Ultimately, it may be necessary to "organize" within the union, and to become an alternative voice. You and like-minded co-workers may need to attend and speak up at union meetings, write letters for publication in the union newsletter, and actively campaign to turn things around. You may end up deciding to run yourself for union office, and to engage in one-on-one organizing to "get out the vote."

No person is perfect, and no society is perfect, either. But all of us are capable of becoming better people than we are today, and we all strive to do so.

Similarly, no matter how messy things may sometimes appear to be in the larger society, we try to bring about improvements to make things better for all.

And our unions are no different. Like the people we know or the society we live in, no union is perfect. But all are capable of improving.

Unions are every working person's best defense against employer excesses, and they are the way our collective voice is heard. Take what you have learned from this book, and use it as a starting point to become a voice and presence in your union. The union is you and your co-workers; you have it within your power to make your union an ever-more-effective fighter for workplace rights and justice.

GLOSSARY

The world of unions has its own vocabulary. Some words or phrases are used solely within this world, while others may have a slightly different meaning than when you encounter them elsewhere. Here is a list of some of the more important parts of the union vocabulary. For a more comprehensive guide to labor terms see *The Lexicon of Labor* by R. Emmett Murray (New York: The New Press, 1998).

AFL-CIO: the national federation that includes most American labor unions, resulting from the 1955 merger of the American Federation of Labor and the Congress of Industrial Organizations.

agency fee: a fee, usually somewhat lower than the full dues amount, that nonmembers are required to pay to the union. The payment is calculated to cover the costs of the representation services that the union provides.

agency shop: *see* union shop

arbitration: the process by which a neutral outside party acts as a "judge," taking evidence and issuing a binding ruling on a contract grievance or other dispute.

bargaining: the process of face-to-face meetings, exchange of proposals, and give and take that produces a union contract.

bargaining team: the union or employer group of individuals that goes to the bargaining table for formal negotiations.

bargaining unit: the group of employees represented by a particular union, and usually covered by a single union contract.

Beck *decision:* a United States Supreme Court decision setting forth the financial rights (and obligations) of agency fee payers.

branch: see union local

Central Labor Councils: the AFL-CIO–sponsored collection of the local unions in a particular city or other geographical area.

chapter: see union local

collective bargaining: see bargaining

collective bargaining agreement: the document produced as a result of negotiations between a union and an employer, constituting the set of binding workplace rules.

constitution and bylaws: the governing documents of a local union or higher up union body.

contract: see collective bargaining agreement

corporate campaign: a multifaceted pressure campaign waged by a union, designed to exploit an employer's legal weaknesses, public relations vulnerabilities, or business bottom line.

dues: the money paid by union members to finance the costs of running the union.

duty of fair representation (DFR): the union's obligation to act diligently and fairly in the interests of members of the bargaining unit. This flows from the union's role as the exclusive representative of all those in the bargaining unit.

enabling legislation: a law that grants the right to unionize to public sector employees.

Equal Employment Opportunity Commission (EEOC): the federal agency that implements many discrimination laws. Many states and localities have equivalent agencies.

Employee Retirement Income Security Act (ERISA): the law governing most private employers' pension and welfare benefit plans.

Fair Labor Standards Act (FLSA): the federal law setting the minimum wage and establishing standards for overtime pay. Many states and localities also have laws applicable in their jurisdictions.

Family and Medical Leave Act (FMLA): the 1993 law creating an entitlement to unpaid leave connected with family emergencies and medical situations.

Federal Labor Relations Authority: the equivalent of the National Labor Relations Board for federal sector employees, administering the federal labor law as it applies to those employed by the federal government.

good cause: see just cause

grandfathering: when there is a change in a workplace rule or job benefit, but employees already on board are permitted to remain under the old rule.

grievance procedure: a series of steps set forth in a union contract for attempting to resolve disputes between the employer and employees/the union.

impasse: a deadlock in contract negotiations.

interest-based bargaining (IBB): an alternative form of negotiations, premised on jointly identifying problems and then finding solutions that benefit both sides.

International: usually refers to the national level of an American union, as in International Brotherhood of Teamsters, so named because of members in Puerto Rico, Canada, or elsewhere.

International Trade Secretariats: the international organizations that coordinate the efforts of the various unions worldwide that represent employees in particular industries or types of work.

just cause: the usual standard for discipline, requiring sufficient and fair grounds before punishing an employee.

Labor Management Reporting and Disclosure Act (LMRDA): a federal law containing the Bill of Rights of Members of Labor Organizations, guaranteeing the right of union members to participate in union meetings, to vote in union elections, and so on.

lodge: see union local

lockout: a refusal by an employer to allow employees to report to work, designed to force the union to accept the employer's position in a bargaining dispute.

mediation: the process by which a neutral person attempts to help the union and an employer resolve a bargaining or other dispute.

mutual-gains bargaining: see interest-based bargaining

National Labor Relations Board (NLRB): the federal agency that administers the National Labor Relations Act, the labor law that applies to most private sector employees. *See also* Wagner Act.

negotiated agreement: see collective bargaining agreement

negotiating team: see bargaining team

negotiations: see bargaining

Occupational Safety and Health Administration (OSHA): the federal agency that administers the basic health and safety law, the Occupational Safety and Health Act.

open shop: a workplace where union membership and payment of dues or other fees to the union are voluntary.

organizing: "external organizing" refers to acquiring union rights for unrepresented employees; "internal organizing" means persuading nonmembers to join the union that already represents them.

past practice: a procedure or workplace custom that can acquire binding effect.

private sector: privately owned companies and their employees.

public sector: government employment at all levels, including state, county, city and other localities.

Railway Labor Act: the labor law covering the transportation industry, with rules on organizing and bargaining that differ substantially from those of the National Labor Relations Act.

rank and file: the members of a union; not the leaders, just you and your co-workers.

ratification: the procedure in which union members vote to accept or reject a negotiated contract settlement.

receiverships: see trusteeships

redcircling: see grandfathering

retaliation: punitive action taken against an employee for exercising a contractual or legal right.

"right to work": legislation prohibiting various types of union security arrangements. In jurisdictions covered by such laws, unions cannot require nonmembers to make a financial payment to cover any of the union's costs of operation.

steward: the front-line union representative, usually a volunteer, who is responsible for giving guidance on workplace rights, filing grievances, and other representation and organizing tasks. Sometimes called "the union's eyes and ears."

seniority: a worker's length of service with an employer relative to the length of service of other workers. Contracts frequently use seniority to determine layoffs, promotions, recalls and transfers.

strike: a collective refusal to work, designed to pressure an employer to accept the union's position in a bargaining or other dispute.

trusteeship: placing the day-to-day running of a union local in the hands of a higher union body, usually as a result of financial irregularities or mismanagement.

unfair labor practice (ULP): a labor law violation, committed by either an employer or a union. Common employer violations include making changes in the workplace without going through the union, and interfering with employees' rights to engage in union activity.

union contract: *see* collective bargaining agreement

union local: the lowest level in a union's formal organizational structure, usually consisting of employees in a particular workplace or city.

union shop ("agency shop"): workplaces where new employees are required either to join the union or to pay a "fair share" fee to the union to compensate it for direct representation and other services.

Wagner Act: the 1935 federal statute, subsequently amended, that set up the framework for union representation for most private sector employees. Formally, the National Labor Relations Act, named for U.S. Senator Robert F. Wagner of New York (1877–1953).

Weingarten *rights:* an employee's right to have a representative present when being questioned about a possible disciplinary infraction. Named for a 1975 United States Supreme Court decision, *NLRB* v. *J. Weingarten, Inc.*

whistleblower: an employee who gives information to the public, the news media, or a government agency about some employer activity that the employee believes is illegal or improper.

win-win bargaining: *see* interest-based bargaining

workers' compensation: the government-regulated insurance scheme providing for set monetary payments to employees who are injured or disabled in connection with their jobs.

HELPFUL CONTACTS

This book, I hope, has made you interested in learning more about unions and workplace rights or in becoming more active in the union movement. Your own union is the best place to start, but there are many other groups to learn from and get materials from. The following list offers a broad sampling of the possibilities.

AFL-CIO
The nation's primary labor federation; links to affiliated unions
815 16th St., N.W.
Washington, DC 20006
Phone: (202) 637-5000
www.aflcio.org

American Civil Liberties Union
Information on workplace rights
125 Broad St., 18th Floor
New York, NY 10004
Phone: (212) 549-2500
www.aclu.org

A. Philip Randolph Institute
African-American unionists
1444 Eye St., N.W., 3rd Floor
Washington, DC 20005
Phone: (202) 289-2774
Fax: (202) 289-5289
www.aprihq.org

Asian Pacific American Labor Alliance
Asian Pacific unionists
815 16th St., N.W.
Washington, DC 20006
Phone: (202) 842-1263
Fax: (202) 842-1462
www.apalanet.org

Association for Union Democracy
Internal union democracy
500 State St.
Brooklyn, NY 11217
Phone: (718) 855-6650
Fax: (718) 855-6799
www.uniondemocracy.org

Coalition of Black Trade Unionists
African-American unionists
PO Box 66268
Washington, DC 20035
Phone: (202) 429-1203
Fax: (202) 429-1102
www.cbtu.org

Coalition of Labor Union Women
Women unionists
1126 16th St., N.W.
Washington, DC 20036
Phone: (202) 466-4610
Fax: (202) 776-0537
www.cluw.org

Department of Labor
Wages and hours, family and medical leave, plant closings
200 Constitution Ave., N.W.
Washington, DC 20210
Phone: (202) 219-6666

www.dol.gov

Equal Employment Opportunity Commission
Discrimination
1801 L St., N.W.
Washington, DC 20507
Phone: (202) 663-4900
www.eeoc.gov

Federal Labor Relations Authority
Unfair labor practices, union representation elections for federal employees
607 14th St., N.W., Suite 210
Washington, DC 20424
Phone: (202) 482-6690
www.flra.gov

George Meany Center for Labor Studies
National labor studies program, including bachelor's and master's degrees
10000 New Hampshire Avenue
Silver Spring, MD 20903
Phone: (301) 431-5422
Fax: (301) 431-5411
www.georgemeany.org

Government Accountability Project
Whistleblower protection group
1612 K St., N.W.
Washington, DC 20006
Phone: (202) 408-0034
www.whistleblower.org

Jewish Labor Committee
Jewish unionists
25 East 21st St.
New York, NY 10010-6207
Phone: (212) 477-0707
Fax: (212) 477-1918

Jobs With Justice
Coalition efforts for workers' rights campaigns
501 3rd St., N.W.
Washington, DC 20001
Phone: (202) 434-1106
www.igc.org/jwj

Labor Council for Latin American Advancement
Latin American unionists
815 16th St., N.W.
Washington, DC 20006
Phone: (202) 347-4223
Fax: (202) 347-5095
www.lclaa.org

Labor Heritage Foundation
Music and arts for the union cause
888 16th St., N.W., 6th Floor
Washington, DC 20006
Phone: (202) 974-8040
www.laborheritage.org

Labornet
Independent information source for labor news and views
www.labornet.org

Labor Notes
News of rank-and-file activism
7435 Michigan Ave.
Detroit, MI 48210
Phone: (313) 842-6262
www.labornotes.org

Labor Research Association
News and analysis covering the labor movement and the economy
145 West 28th St.
New York, NY 10001

Phone: (212) 714-1677
www.laborresearch.org

Legal Information Institute
Links to employment and labor laws of all fifty states, the District of Columbia and Puerto Rico
www.law.cornell.edu/topics/Table_Labor.htm

National Employment Lawyers Association
Links to labor law sites
www.nela.org

National Labor Relations Board
Unfair labor practices, union representation elections for private sector employees
1099 14th St., N.W.
Washington, DC 20570
Phone: (202) 273-1000
www.nlrb.gov

Northland Poster Collective
Buttons, posters, you name it—most with a union theme
PO Box 7096
Minneapolis, MN 55407
Phone: (800) 627-3082
Fax: (612) 721-2160
www.northlandposter.com

Occupational Safety and Health Administration
Health and safety
U.S. Department of Labor
200 Constitution Ave., N.W.
Washington, DC 20210
Phone: (800) 356-4674
www.osha.gov

Pride At Work
Mutual support between the labor movement and the gay, lesbian and

137

transgender community
815 16th St., N.W., Room 4020
Washington, DC 20006
Phone: (202) 637-5085
Fax: (202) 508-6923
www.prideatwork.org

Union Communication Services, Inc.

Books, communications and educational tools for activist union leaders; publishers of this book
165 Conduit St.
Annapolis, MD 21401
Phone: (800) 321-2545
Fax: (410) 626-1353
www.unionist.com

Union Jobs Clearinghouse

Job openings in the labor movement
www.unionjobs.com

Union Label Department, AFL-CIO

Information on union-made products and services
815 16th St., N.W.
Washington, DC 20006
Phone: (202) 628-2131
www.unionlabel.org

Union Privilege

Labor-sponsored credit cards, auto club, etc.
1125 15th St., N.W., Suite 300
Washington, DC 20005
Phone: (202) 293-5330
Fax: (202) 293-5311
www.unionpriv.org

DIRECTORY OF UNIONS

The following list gives contact information on all major unions in the United States, including every one affiliated with the AFL-CIO, and many—but not all—of the country's independent unions, as well as some other related organizations and professional associations.

Actors & Artistes of America, Associated (AAAA)
165 West 46th St., Suite 500
New York, NY 10036
Phone: (212) 869-0358
Fax: (212) 869-1746

Actors' Equity Association
165 West 46th St.
New York, NY 10036
Phone: (212) 869-8530
Fax: (212) 719-9815
www.actorsequity.org

Airline Pilots Association (ALPA)
1625 Massachusetts Ave., N.W.
Washington, DC 20036
Phone: (202) 797-4010
Fax: (202) 797-4052
www.alpa.org

American Association of University Professors (AAUP)
1012 14th St., N.W., Suite 500
Washington, DC 20005
Phone: (202) 737-5900
Fax: (202) 737-5526
E-mail: aaup@aaup.org
www.aaup.org

American Federation of Television & Radio Artists (AFTRA)
260 Madison Ave.
New York, NY 10016
Phone: (212) 532-0800
Fax: (212) 532-2242
www.aftra.org

American Guild of Musical Artists (AGMA)
1727 Broadway
New York, NY 10019
Phone: (212) 265-3687
Fax: (212) 262-9088
www.musicalartists.org

American Guild of Variety Artists (AGVA)
184 Fifth Ave.
New York, NY 10010
Phone: (212) 675-1003

American Nurses' Association (ANA)
600 Maryland Ave., S.W., Suite 100 West
Washington, DC 20024-2571
Phone: (202) 651-7000
Fax: (202) 651-7001
www.nursingworld.org

Asbestos Workers, International Association of (AWIU)

1776 Massachusetts Ave., N.W., Suite 301
Washington, DC 20036
Phone: (202) 785-2388
Fax: (202) 429-0568
E-mail: iiiaft@aol.com
www.insulators.org

Automobile, Aerospace & Agricultural Implement Workers of America (UAW)
8000 E. Jefferson Ave.
Detroit, MI 48214
Phone: (313) 926-5000
Fax: (313) 823-6016
E-mail: uaw@uaw.org
www.uaw.org

Bakery, Confectionary, Tobacco Workers and Grain Millers International Union (BCTGM)
10401 Connecticut Ave.
Kensington, MD 20895
Phone: (301) 933-8600
Fax: (301) 946-8452
www.bctgm.org

Boilermakers, Iron Ship Builders, Blacksmiths, Forgers and Helpers (IBB)
753 State Ave., Suite 570
Kansas City, KS 66101
Phone: (913) 371-2640
Fax: (913) 281-8101
www.boilermakers.org

Bricklayers and Allied Craftworkers, International Union of (BAC)
815 15th St., N.W.
Washington, DC 20005
Phone: (202) 783-3788

Fax: (202) 393-3103
www.bacweb.org

California School Employees Association (CSEA)
2045 Lundy Ave., PO Box 640
San Jose, CA 95106
Phone: (408) 263-8000
Fax: (408) 954-0948
www.csea.com

Carpenters & Joiners of America, United Brotherhood of (UBC)
101 Constitution Ave., N.W.
Washington, DC 20001
Phone: (202) 546-6206
Fax: (202) 543-5724

Christian Labor Association (CLA)
405 Centerstone Ct., PO Box 65
Zeeland, MI 49464
Phone: (616) 772-9164
Fax: (616) 772-9830
E-mail: chrlabor@eagledesign.com

Communications Workers of America (CWA)
501 3rd St., N.W.
Washington, DC 20001
Phone: (202) 434-1100
Fax: (202) 434-1375
E-mail: cwa@cwa-union.org
www.cwa-union.org

Electrical Workers, International Brotherhood of (IBEW)
1125 15th St., N.W.

Washington, DC 20005
Phone: (202) 833-7000
Fax: (202) 728-7664
www.ibew.org

Elevator Constructors, International Union of (IUEC)
5565 Sterrett Pl.
Columbia, MD 21044
Phone: (410) 997-9000
Fax: (410) 997-0243
E-mail: info@iuec.org
www.iuec.org

Farm Workers of America, United (UFW)
29700 Woodford-Tehachapi Rd.
Keene, CA 93531
Phone: (661) 822-5571
Fax: (661) 822-6103
E-mail: execoffice@ufwmail.com
www.ufw.org

Fire Fighters, International Association of (IAFF)
1750 New York Ave., N.W.
Washington, DC 20006
Phone: (202) 737-8484
Fax: (202) 737-8418
www.iaff.org

Flight Attendants, Association of (AFA)
1275 K St., N.W., 5th Floor
Washington, DC 20005
Phone: (202) 712-9799
Fax: (202) 712-9798
E-mail: afatalk@afanet.org
www.flightattendant-afa.org

Flight Engineers' International Association (FEIA)
1926 Pacific Coast Hwy., Suite 202
Redondo Beach, CA 90277
Phone: (310) 316-4094
Fax: (310) 316-6167

Food and Commercial Workers International Union, United (UFCW)
1775 K St., N.W.
Washington, DC 20006
Phone: (202) 223-3111
Fax: (202) 466-1562
E-mail: voice@ufcw.org
www.ufcw.org

Fraternal Order of Police (FOP)
1410 Donelson Pike, Suite A-17
Nashville, TN 37217
Phone: (615) 399-0900
Fax: (615) 399-0400
E-mail: glfop@grandlodgefop.org
www.grandlodgefop.org

Glass Workers Union, American Flint (AFGWU)
1440 South Byrne Rd.
Toledo, OH 43614
Phone: (419) 385-6687
Fax: (419) 385-8839
E-mail: dlusetti@netzero.net

Glass, Molders, Pottery, Plastics & Allied Workers International Union (GMP)
608 East Baltimore Pike
Media, PA 19063
Phone: (610) 565-5051
Fax: (610) 565-0983

E-mail: gmpiu@ix.netcom.com
www.gmpiu.org

Government Employees, American Federation of (AFGE)
80 F St., N.W.
Washington, DC 20001
Phone: (202) 737-8700
Fax: (202) 639-6490
www.afge.org

Graphic Artists Guild
90 John St., Suite 403
New York, NY 10038-3202
Phone: (212) 791-3400
Fax: (212) 791-0333
E-mail: paulatgag@aol.com
www.gag.org

Graphic Communications International Union (GCIU)
1900 L St., N.W.
Washington, DC 20036-4804
Phone: (202) 462-1400
Fax: (202) 331-9516
www.gciu.org

Health & Human Service Employees Union, National
310 West 43rd St.
New York, NY 10036
Phone: (212) 582-1890
Fax: (212) 956-5140
www.1199.org

Horseshoers of US and Canada, International Union of Journeymen
6920 Hitchcock Rd.
White Lake, MI 48383

Phone: (810) 887-5922

Hotel Employees & Restaurant Employees International Union (HEREIU)
1219 28th St., N.W.
Washington, DC 20007
Phone: (202) 393-4373
Fax: (202) 333-0468
www.hereunion.org

Independent Pilots Association (IPA)
200 Highrise Dr., Suite 199
Louisville, KY 40213
Phone: (502) 968-0341
Fax: (502) 515-1426
www.ipapilot.org

International Union of Security Officers (IUSO)
2404 Merced St.
San Leandro, CA 94577
Phone: (510) 895-9905
Fax: (510) 895-6974

Iron Workers, International Association of Bridge, Structural & Ornamental
1750 New York Ave., N.W., Suite 400
Washington, DC 20006
Phone: (202) 383-4800
Fax: (202) 638-4856

Laborers' International Union of North America (LIUNA)
905 16th St., N.W.
Washington, DC 20006
Phone: (202) 737-8320
Fax: (202) 737-2754
www.liuna.org

Letter Carriers, National Association of (NALC)
100 Indiana Ave., N.W.
Washington, DC 20001
Phone: (202) 393-4695
Fax: (202) 737-1540
www.nalc.org

Locomotive Engineers, Brotherhood of (BLE)
Standard Building, Mezzanine Level
1370 Ontario Ave.
Cleveland, OH 44113
Phone: (216) 241-2630
Fax: (216) 241-6516
E-mail: bennett@ble.org
www.ble.org

Longshoremen's and Warehousemen's Union, International (ILWU)
1188 Franklin St.
San Francisco, CA 94109-6800
Phone: (415) 775-0533
Fax: (415) 775-1302
www.ilwu.org

Longshoremen's Association, International (ILA)
17 Battery Pl., Suite 930
New York, NY 10004
Phone: (212) 425-1200
Fax: (212) 425-2928
www.ilaunion.org

Machinists and Aerospace Workers, International Association of (IAM)
9000 Machinists Pl.
Upper Marlboro, MD 20772
Phone: (301) 967-4500
Fax: (301) 967-4515
www.iamaw.org

Maintenance of Way Employees, Brotherhood of (BWE)
26555 Evergreen Rd, Suite 200
Southfield, MI 48076
Phone: (248) 948-1010
Fax: (248) 948-7150
www.bmwe.org

Marine Engineers' Beneficial Association (MEBA)
444 North Capitol St., N.W., Suite 800
Washington, DC 20001
Phone: (202) 638-5355
Fax: (202) 638-5369
E-mail: mebahq@d1meba.org
www.d1meba.org

Maryland Classified Employees Association, Inc. (MCEA)
7127 Rutherford Rd.
Baltimore, MD 21207
Phone: (410) 298-8800
Fax: (410) 298-8058
www.mcea.org

Mine Workers of America, United (UMWA)
8315 Lee Hwy.
Fairfax, VA 22031
Phone: (703) 208-7200
Fax: (703) 208-7227
www.umwa.org

Montana Public Employees Association, Inc. (MONT-PEA)
PO Box 5600
Helena, MT 59604
Phone: (406) 442-4600
Fax: (406) 442-3665

Musicians of the US and Canada, American Federation of (AFM)
1501 Broadway, Suite 600
New York, NY 10036
Phone: (212) 869-1330
Fax: (212) 764-6134
E-mail: pressoffice@afm.org
www.afm.org

National Alliance of Postal and Federal Employees (NAPFE)
1628 11th St., N.W.
Washington, DC 20001
Phone: (202) 939-6325
Fax: (202) 939-6389
E-mail: napfe@patriot.net
www.napfe.com

National Education Association (NEA)
1201 16th St., N.W.
Washington, DC 20036
Phone: (202) 833-4000
Fax: (202) 822-7206
www.nea.org

National Federation of Federal Employees (NFFE)
1016 16th St., N.W.
Washington, DC 20036
Phone: (202) 862-4400
Fax: (202) 862-4432
E-mail: nffehq@erols.com
www.nffe.org

National Maritime Union (NMU)
1150 17th St., N.W., Suite 700
Washington, DC 20036-4614

Phone: (202) 466-7060
Fax: (202) 872-0912
www.nmuhou.org

National Rural Letter Carriers' Association (NRLCA)
1630 Duke St., 4th Floor
Alexandria, VA 22314-3465
Phone: (703) 684-5545
Fax: (703) 548-8735
www.nrlca.org

National Treasury Employees Union (NTEU)
901 E St., N.W., Suite 600
Washington, DC 20004
Phone: (202) 783-4444
Fax: (202) 783-4085
E-mail: nteu-info@nteu.org
www.nteu.org

Novelty and Production Workers, International Union of Allied
1950 West Erie St.
Chicago, IL 60622
Phone: (312) 738-0822
Fax: (312) 738-3553

National Air Traffic Controllers Association (NATCA)
1325 Massachusetts Ave., N.W.
Washington, DC 20005
Phone: (202) 628-5451
Fax: (202) 628-5767
E-mail: ccannon@natcadc.org
www.natcadc.org

Office and Professional Employees International Union (OPEIU)

265 West 14th St., Suite 610
New York, NY 10011
Phone: (212) 675-3210
Fax: (212) 727-3466
E-mail: opeiu@opeiu.org
www.opeiu.org

Operating Engineers, International Union of (IUOE)
1125 17th St., N.W.
Washington, DC 20036
Phone: (202) 429-9100
Fax: (202) 778-2619
www.iuoe.org

Oregon School Employees Association (OSEA)
4735 Liberty Rd. South, P.O. Box 4027
Salem, OR 97302
Phone: (503) 588-0121
Fax: (503) 588-8307
E-mail: osea@worldnet.att.net
www.osea.org

Paper, Allied-Industrial, Chemical Employees International Union (PACE)
3340 Perimeter Hill Dr.
Nashville, TN 37211
Phone: (615) 834-8590
Fax: (615) 834-7741
E-mail: 71363.2772@compuserve.com
www.paceunion.org

Painters & Allied Trades of the US & Canada, International Brotherhood of (IBPAT)
1750 New York Ave., N.W.
Washington, DC 20006

Phone: (202) 637-0700
Fax: (202) 637-0771
E-mail: mail@iupat.org
www.iupat.org

Plasterers' & Cement Masons' International Association of the US & Canada, Operative (OP+CMIA)
14405 Laurel Pl., #300
Laurel, MD 20707-6102
Phone: (301) 470-4200
Fax: (301) 470-2502
E-mail: opcmiaintl@opcmia.org
www.opcmia.org

Plate Printers, Die Stampers & Engravers Union of North America
14th and C St., S.W.
Washington, DC 20228
Phone: (202) 874-2554
Fax: (202) 874-1187

United Association of Plumbing and Pipefitting Industry (UA)
901 Massachusetts Ave., N.W.
Washington, DC 20001
Phone: (202) 628-5823
(202) 628-5024
E-mail: martym@uanet.org
www.ua.org

Police Associations, International Union of (IUPA)
1421 Prince St., Suite 330
Alexandria, VA 22314
Phone: (703) 549-7473
Fax: (703) 683-9048

www.iupa.org

Postal Workers Union, American (APWU)
1300 L St., N.W.
Washington, DC 20005
Phone: (202) 842-4200
Fax: (202) 842-4297
www.apwu.org

Professional and Technical Engineers, International Federation of (IFPTE)
8630 Fenton St., Suite 400
Silver Spring, MD 20910
Phone: (301) 565-9016
Fax: (301) 565-0018
E-mail: www.ifpte.org

Professional Athletes, Federation of
2021 L St., N.W., 6th Floor
Washington. DC 20036
Phone: (202) 463-2200
Fax: (202) 857-0380

Radio Association, American (ARA)
360 West 31st St., 3rd Floor
New York, NY 10001
Phone: (212) 594-3600
Fax: (212) 594-7422
E-mail: arany@mindspring.com

Roofers, Waterproofers and Allied Workers, United Union of
1660 L St., N.W., Suite 800
Washington, DC 20036
Phone: (202) 463-7663

Fax: (202) 463-6906
Web: www.unionroofers.com

School Administrators, American Federation of (AFSA)
1729 21st St., N.W.
Washington, DC 20009
Phone: (202) 986-4209
Fax: (202) 986-4211
E-mail: afsa@admin.org
www.admin.org

Screen Actors Guild (SAG)
5757 Wilshire Blvd.
Los Angeles, CA 90036
Phone: (213) 954-1600
Fax: (213) 549-6603
www.sag.com

Seafarers International Union of North America (SIU)
5201 Auth Way and Britannia Way
Camp Springs, MD 20746
Phone: (301) 899-0675
Fax: (301) 899-7355
www.seafarers.org

Service Employees International Union (SEIU)
1313 I. St., N.W.
Washington, DC 20005
Phone:(202) 898-3200
Fax: (202) 898-3402
E-mail: info@seiu.org
www.seiu.org

Sheet Metal Workers International

Association (SMWIA)
1750 New York Ave., N.W.
Washington, DC 20006
Phone: (202) 783-5880
Fax: (202) 662-0894
www.smwia.org

Signalmen, Brotherhood of Railroad (BRS)
601 West Golf Rd., PO Box "U"
Mount Prospect, IL 60056
Phone: (847) 439-3732
Fax: (847) 439-3743
E-mail: signal@brs.org
www.brs.org

South Dakota State Employees Organization (SD-SEO)
PO Box 1021
Pierre, SD 57501
Phone: (605) 224-8241
Fax: (605) 945-0417
E-mail: info@sdseo.org
www.sdseo.org

Stage Employees & Moving Picture Techs, Artists & Allied Crafts (IATSE)
1515 Broadway, Ste. 601
New York, NY 10036
Phone: (212) 730-1770
Fax: (212) 921-7699
www.iatse.lm.com

State Employees Association of North Carolina, Inc. (SEANC)
PO Drawer 27727
Raleigh, NC 27611

Phone: (919) 833-6436
Fax: (919) 829-5829
www.seanc.org

State, County and Municipal Employees, American Federation of (AFSCME)
1625 L St., N.W.
Washington, DC 20036
Phone: (202) 429-1000
Fax: (202) 429-1102
www.afscme.org

Steelworkers of America, United (USWA)
Five Gateway Center
Pittsburgh, PA 15222
Phone: (412) 562-2300
Fax: (412) 562-2598
www.uswa.org

Teachers, American Federation of (AFT)
555 New Jersey Ave., N.W.
Washington, DC 20001
Phone: (202) 879-4400
Fax: (202) 638-2589
E-mail: online@aft.org
www.aft.org

Teamsters, International Brotherhood of (IBT)
25 Louisiana Ave., N.W.
Washington, DC 20001
Phone: (202) 624-6800
Fax: (202) 624-8102
www.teamsters.org

Train Dispatchers, American
1370 Ontario St., Suite 1040

Cleveland, OH 44113
Phone: (216) 241-2770
Fax: (216) 241-6286
E-mail: atddble@aol.com
www.atdd.org

Transit Union, Amalgamated (ATU)
5025 Wisconsin Ave., N.W., 3rd Floor
Washington, DC 20016
Phone: (202) 537-1645
Fax: (202) 244-7824
www.atu.org

Transport Workers Union of America (TWU)
80 West End Ave., 5th Floor
New York, NY 10023
Phone: (212) 873-6000
Fax: (212) 721-1431
www.twu.org

Transportation • Communications International Union (TCU)
3 Research Pl.
Rockville, MD 20850
Phone: (301) 948-4910
Fax: (301) 948-1369
www.tcunion.org

Transportation Union, United (UTU)
14600 Detroit Ave.
Cleveland, OH 44107
Phone: (216) 228-9400
Fax: (216) 228-5755
www.utu.org

Union of Needletrades, Industrial and

Textile Employees (UNITE)
1710 Broadway
New York, NY 10019
Phone: (212) 265-7000
Fax: (212) 315-3803
E-mail: webmaster@uniteunion.org
www.uniteunion.org

**United Electrical, Radio and Machine
Workers of America (UE)**
One Gateway Ctr., Suite 1400
Pittsburgh, PA 15222-1416
Phone: (412) 471-8919
Fax: (412) 471-8999
E-mail: ue@ranknfile-ue.org
www.ranknfile-ue.org

Utah Public Employees' Association (UPEA)
1000 W Bellwood Ln.
Murray, UT 84123
Phone: (801) 264-8732
Fax: (801) 264-8879
www.upea.net

Utah School Employees Association (USEA)
864 East Arrowhead Ln.
Murray, UT 84107-5211
Phone: (801) 269-9320
Fax: (801) 269-9324
www.useautah.org

Utility Workers Union of America (UWUA)
815 16th St., N.W., Suite 605
Washington, DC 20006
Phone: (202) 347-8105
Fax: (202) 347-4872
E-mail: 71112.2131@compuserve.com
www.uwua.org

INDEX

A

A. Philip Randolph Institute, 133
ACLU (American Civil Liberties
    Union), 133
Actors & Artistes of America,
    Associated (AAAA), 139
Actors' Equity Association, 139
ADA (Americans with Disabilities
    Act, 1990), 96
administrative employees, FLSA
    and, 95
advisory arbitration, 80
AFA (Flight Attendants,
    Association of), 142
affiliations of unions, 18–19
AFGE (Government Employees,
    American Federation of), 142
AFGWU (Glass Workers Union,
    American Flint), 142
AFL-CIO, 13, 18–19, 125, 133
AFM (Musicians of the US and
    Canada, American Federation
    of), 144
African-Americans. *See also*
    Coalition of Black Trade
    Unionists; A. Philip
    Randolph Institute
    striking sanitation workers, 10
AFSA (School Administrators,
    American Federation of), 147
AFSCME (American Federation of
    State, County and Municipal
    Employees), 10
AFT (Teachers, American
    Federation of), 148

AFTRA (American Federation of
    Television & Radio Artists),
    140
Age Discrimination in
    Employment Act (1967), 96
agency fees, 26–28, 125
agency shop, 26, 130
AGMA (American Guild of
    Musical Artists), 140
agricultural workers, 92, 93. *See
    also* farmworkers
AGVA (American Guild of Variety
    Artists), 140
Airline Pilots Association (ALPA),
    139
Amalgamated Clothing and Textile
    Workers Union, 18
American Arbitration Association,
    79
American Association of University
    Professors (AAUP), 21, 140
American Civil Liberties Union
    (ACLU), 133
American Federation of
    Labor–Congress of Industrial
    Organizations. See AFL-CIO
American Federation of State,
    County and Municipal
    Employees (AFSCME), 10
American Federation of Television
    & Radio Artists (AFTRA),
    140
American Guild of Musical Artists
    (AGMA), 140
American Guild of Variety Artists

151

(AGVA), 140
American Nurses' Association (ANA), 140
Americans with Disabilities Act (1990), 96
anti-discrimination statutes, 61
apprenticeship programs, discrimination in, 96
APWU (Postal Workers Union, American), 146
ARA (Radio Association, American), 146
arbitration (grievance), 16, 69, 79–85, 125
  case selection, 83–84
  employers and, 84–85
  hearing, 81–83
  preparation timetable, 80–81
arbitration boards, 79–80
arbitrators
  at arbitration hearing, 82–83
  permanent, 79
  public employees' bargaining and, 49
  selection and duties, 79–80
Asbestos Workers, International Association of (AWIU), 140
Asian Pacific American Labor Alliance, 134
assembly, freedom of, 37–38
assessments, 30
Association for Union Democracy, 134
Athletes, Federation of Professional, 146
ATU (Transit Union, Amalgamated), 148
audits, of union financial information, 28
Automobile, Aerospace & Agricultural Implement Workers of America (UAW), 140

B

Bakery, Confectionary, Tobacco Workers and Grain Millers International Union (BCTGM), 140
bargaining, 125. *See also* collective bargaining agreements; strikes
  contract campaigns, 49–50
  corporate campaigns, 50–51
  deadlock, 47
  employee involvement programs and, 15
  good faith, 51
  interest-based, 52–55
  legal framework for, 51–52
  members' involvement in, 42–43
  procedures, 44–45
  right to information, 52
  surveys, 42–43
  team, 43–44, 126
  unit, 62, 126
Beck decision (1988), 27, 126
benefits, 58–65
bereavement leave, 59
Bill of Rights of Members of Labor Organizations, 37–38
BLE (Locomotive Engineers, Brotherhood of), 143
Boilermakers, Iron Ship Builders, Blacksmiths, Forgers and Helpers (IBB), 140
branch, union, 16
Bricklayers and Allied Craftworkers, International Union of (BAC), 140–141
Broadcast Technicians Union, 18
BRS (Signalmen, Brotherhood of Railroad), 147
buying programs, discount, 8
buyouts, 63
BWE (Maintenance of Way Employees, Brotherhood of), 144

C

California, agricultural workers protections in, 93
California School Employees Association (CSEA), 141
"captive audience" meetings, 112
Carpenters & Joiners of America, United Brotherhood of (UBC), 141
Central Labor Councils, AFL-CIO, 19, 126
chapter, union, 16
checkoff, dues, 30
chief stewards, 16
Christian Labor Association (CLA), 141
Civil Rights Act (1964), Title VII, 95–96
closed shops, 28
closings, business
  laws on, 97
  union organizing and, 112
Coalition of Black Trade Unionists, 134
Coalition of Labor Union Women, 134
collective bargaining agreements, 8–9, 126. *See also* bargaining
  changes to, 64–65
  chargeable expenses for, 27
  duration of, 64
  essential items in, 58–59, 61–64
  fairness in, 26
  health and safety provisions, 63, 98
  on institutional rights of unions, 64
  on job reductions, 63, 65
  on joint labor-management committees, 63–64, 65
  jurisdiction, 62
  omissions, 60
  on personnel records, 64
  printing after ratification, 46–47
  on probationary periods, 63
  for public employees, 58
  ratification, 45–46
  reading, 57
  on retirement options, 63
  scope, 57–65
  stall and delay tactics against,

by employers, 112, 114
tentative, 45
on union membership and
dues, 62
"union security" provisions in,
26
voting rights, 24
workplace rights, 87
committees, union, 16–17
bargaining, 43–44
national, 18
Communications Workers of
America (CWA), 18, 141
compensation. *See* pay
compensatory time, 59
complaints (workplace), alternative
relief for, 36–37, 84
"concerted activities," 91–92
confidential employees, 92
conflicting interests of workers,
balance of, 8, 34, 36
Congress, NLRB and, 92
Constitution, U.S., 100
constitution and bylaws, of unions,
17, 29, 37, 39, 119, 120
defined, 89, 126
consumers, appealing to, 50–51
contract campaigns, 49–50
contracts, union. *See* collective bargaining agreements
cooperation, spirit of, 18–19
interest-based bargaining and,
53
national union organizations,
17–18
regional union organizations,
17
corporate campaigns, 50–51, 126
corruption, trusteeships and, 39
Council of Chapters, 17
counseling services, 64
county unions, 17
credit cards, union, 8
credit unions, 8

D

Davis-Bacon law, 9

deadlock, bargaining, 47
"defined benefits," under ERISA,
100
delay tactics, employer, 112
Department of Labor, U.S.,
134–135
different worker interests, balancing, 8, 34, 36
direct actions, 76–77
discipline, employee, 59, 61–62,
103–107
representation and, 104, 105
retaliation protections,
106–107
disclosure, union financial information, 28
discrimination
EEOC on, 95–96
statutes on, 61
District Council, 17
domestic workers
FLSA and, 95
NLRA and, 92
due process procedures, 62
dues, 28–29, 126
collective bargaining agreements on, 62
determination of, 29
fairness of, 25
increases in, 29–30
initiation fees and assessments,
30
payment mechanics, 30–31
progressive structure, 29
purpose and uses of, 24–25
duty of fair representation (DFR),
33–35, 126

E

economic strikes, 48
education, on union activities,
118–119
education, scheduling time off for,
59
Education International, 21
EEOC. *See* Equal Employment
Opportunity Commission

elections, union officer, 17, 37, 38
Electrical Workers, International
Brotherhood of (IBEW), 141
Electronic Workers Union, 18
Elevator Constructors,
International Union of
(IUEC), 141
employee involvement programs,
15
employee unity, grievances and,
70–71
employers. *See also* joint labor-
management committees
arbitration and, 84–85
bulletin boards, 64, 95, 98–99
enlightened, interest-based
bargaining and, 53
grievance initiation by, 69–70
handbooks and regulations, 88
interests in number of dues-
paying union members, 24
employment at will, 61
employment terms and conditions,
51–52
enabling legislation, 94, 126
entry (initiation) fees, 30
Environmental Protection Agency
(EPA), 98
Equal Employment Opportunity
Commission (EEOC), 95–96,
127, 135
Equal Pay Act (1963), 96
ERISA (Employment Retirement
Income Security Act),
100–101, 127

F

fact-finders, public employees' bargaining and, 48–49
Fair Labor Standards Act (FLSA),
94–95, 127
fair representation. *See* duty of fair
representation (DFR)
fair share fees, 26, 130
Family and Medical Leave Act
(FMLA), 97, 127
family leave, 59

farmworkers. *See also* agricultural workers
  FLSA and, 95
  state protections for, 93
Farm Workers of America, United (UFW), 141
Federal Labor Relations Authority (FLRA), 93, 127, 135
Federal Mediation and Conciliation Service, 79
finances, union
  challenges to expenditures, 28
  information about, 38
Fire Fighters, International Association of (IAFF), 141
firing
  discrimination in, 95–96
  union organizing and, 112
First Amendment, U.S. Constitution, 37
Flight Attendants, Association of (AFA), 142
FLSA. *See* Fair Labor Standards Act
Food and Commercial Workers International Union, United (UFCW), 142
Form 200, OSHA, 99
Fraternal Order of Police (FOP), 142

G
George Meany Center for Labor Studies, 135
Glass, Molders, Pottery, Plastics & Allied Workers International Union (GMP), 142
Glass Workers Union, American Flint (AFGWU), 142
Gompers, Samuel, 21
"good cause," for discipline, 61, 127
good faith bargaining, 51
governing body, national union, 17
Government Accountability Project, 135
Government Employees, American

Federation of (AFGE), 142
government laws and regulations. *See* labor law
"grandfathering," 59, 127
Graphic Artists Guild, 142
Graphic Communications International Union (GCIU), 142
grievances, 15, 16. *See also* arbitration
  DFR and, 34–35
  direct action and, 76–77
  due process and, 62
  eligibility for filing, 69–70
  group, 75, 83
  initiation factors, 71–72
  members' role in, 73–74, 81, 82
  priorities for, 84
  reasons for, 70–71
  relief availability under, 74–75
  scope of, 67–69
  steps in, 72–73
  strategic use of, 84
  tactical uses of, 75–76

H
Hawaii, agricultural workers protections in, 93
hazardous materials and conditions, 99
health and safety, 8
  contract provisions, 63, 68, 98
  laws, 98–100
  mandatory bargaining on, 51–52
Health & Human Service Employees Union, National, 142
hearings, arbitration, 81–83. *See also* arbitration (grievance); grievances
hiring
  discrimination in, 95–96
  union halls for, 28
holidays observed, 59
holiday work, 59, 95

Holmes, Oliver Wendell, 25
Horseshoers of US and Canada, International Union of Journeymen, 142–143
Hotel Employees & Restaurant Employees International Union (HEREIU), 143
hours of work, 51–52
  labor laws on, 94–95
Hughes, Charles Evans, 5

I
IAFF (Fire Fighters, International Association of), 141
IAM (Machinists and Aerospace Workers, International Association of), 143
IATSE (Stage Employees & Moving Picture Techs, Artists & Allied Crafts), 148
IBB (Boilermakers, Iron Ship Builders, Blacksmiths, Forgers and Helpers), 140
IBEW (Electrical Workers, International Brotherhood of), 141
IBPAT (Painters & Allied Trades of the US & Canada, International Brotherhood of), 146
IBT (Teamsters, International Brotherhood of), 13, 20, 148
identification tag rules, 64
IFPTE (Professional and Technical Engineers, International Federation of), 146
ILA (Longshoremen's Association, International), 143
ILWU (Longshoremen's and Warehousemen's Union International), 143
immigration laws, 101
impasse, in contract negotiations, 47, 127
independent contractors, NLRA and, 92
Independent Pilots Association

(IPA), 143
India, United Parcel Service strike (1997) and, 20
initiation fees and assessments, 30
injuries, OSHA Form 200 on, 99
insubordination, 68
interest-based bargaining (IBB), 52–53, 127
  dangers, 54–55
  description, 53–54
international (union organizations), 17, 128
International Confederation of Free Trade Unions (ICFTU), 21
International Labor Organization (ILO), 21
International Ladies Garment Workers Union (ILGWU), 18
international trade policies, 19–21
International Trade Secretariats, 20, 21, 128
International Transport Workers Federation, 20
International Typographical Union, 18
International Union of Food, Agricultural, Hotel, Restaurant, Catering, Tobacco and Allied Workers' Associations (IUF), 21
International Union of Security Officers (IUSO), 143
Internet Service Providers, 8–9
interstate commerce, NLRA and, 92
intimidation campaigns, union organizing and, 112
investigatory interviews, 104
Iron Workers, International Association of Bridge, Structural & Ornamental, 143
IUEC (Elevator Constructors, International Union of), 141
IUOE (Operating Engineers, International Union of), 145

IUPA (Police Associations, International Union of), 146

J
Jewish Labor Committee, 135
job applicants, discrimination against, 95
job reductions, 63, 65
job security, 59, 65
Jobs With Justice, 136
job training, discrimination in, 96
joint labor-management committees, 16, 63–64, 65
jury duty, 59
"just cause," for discipline, 61, 128

K
Kennedy, John F., 93
King, Martin Luther, Jr., 9–10

L
Labor, U.S. Department of, 134–135
  Fair Labor Standards Act (FLSA), 94–95, 127
  FMLA claims, 97
  Labor-Management (LM) reports and, 38
  LMRDA enforcement, 39
Labor Council for Latin American Advancement, 136
Laborers' International Union of North America (LIUNA), 143
Labor Heritage Foundation, 136
labor law
  on business closings, 97
  on contract negotiations, 51–52
  on discrimination, 95–96
  on family and medical leave, 97
  federal, on pensions, 100–101
  FLRA, 93–94
  on health and safety, 98–100
  on immigration, 101
  local, 93–94

NLRA, 90–93
  for public sector workers, 90–93
  for private sector workers, 93–94
  state, 93–94, 98
  on union membership, 26–28
  on union operations, 17
  on veterans and reservists, 97–98
  on wages and hours, 94–95
  on whistleblowing, 100
  on workers' compensation, 101, 137
  on workplace issues, 9
  workplace rights and, 88
labor-management relations
  information about, 25
  joint committees, 16, 63–64, 65
Labor Management Reporting and Disclosure Act (LMRDA), 37, 128
Labor-Management (LM) reports, 38
Labornet, 136
Labor Notes, 136
Labor Research Association, 136–137
Landrum-Griffin Act, 37
law, workplace. *See* collective bargaining agreement; labor law
"law of the shop," 88
leave policies
  in collective bargaining agreements, 59
  labor laws on, 97
  mandatory bargaining on, 51–52
Legal Information Institute, 137
legislation. *See* labor law
Letter Carriers, National Association of (NALC), 143
litigation, anti-union, 27
"living wage," 95
lobbying expenses, agency fees and, 28

local, union. *See* union local
lockouts, 47, 128
Locomotive Engineers,
    Brotherhood of (BLE), 143
lodge, union, 16. *See also* union
    local
Log and Summary of Occupational
    Injuries (OSHA Form 200),
    99
Longshoremen's and
    Warehousemen's Union
    International (ILWU), 143
Longshoremen's Association,
    International (ILA), 143
Ludlow Massacre, 113

M

Machinists and Aerospace
    Workers, International
    Association of (IAM), 143
"maintenance of membership," 26
Maintenance of Way Employees,
    Brotherhood of (BWE), 144
management rights, in grievances,
    68
managers, NLRA exclusion of, 92
March on Washington for Jobs and
    Freedom (1963), 10
Marine Engineers' Beneficial
    Association (MEBA), 144
Maryland Classified Employees
    Association, Inc. (MCEA),
    144
mass-filing of grievances, 75–76,
    83
Meany (George) Center for Labor
    Studies, 135
mediation, 128
mediators, 47, 48–49
medical leave
    collective bargaining agree-
        ments on, 59
    labor laws on, 97
members/membership, 26
    collective bargaining agree-
        ments on, 62
    grievance initiation by, 69

grievance procedure role,
    73–74, 81, 82
interest-based bargaining and,
    54–55
objections to, 27
rationales for and against, 8–9,
    23–27
rights and responsibilities,
    23–31
rights, violations of, 35–37,
    38–39
roles of, 117–123
union security, 23–26
mergers
    corporate, seniority lists in, 8
    of unions, 18
merit pay determination, 58
mileage reimbursements, 59
Mine Workers of America, United
    (UMWA), 113, 144
Montana Public Employees
    Association, Inc. (MONT-
    PEA), 144
municipal unions, 17
Musicians of the US and Canada,
    American Federation of
    (AFM), 144
mutual-gains bargaining, 52, 128.
    See also interest-based bar-
    gaining

N

NAFTA (North American Free
    Trade Agreement), 21
NALC (Letter Carriers, National
    Association of), 143
name badges, 64
National Air Traffic Controllers
    Association (NATCA), 145
National Alliance of Postal and
    Federal Employees (NAPFE),
    144
National Education Association
    (NEA), 19, 21, 144
National Employment Lawyers
    Association, 137
National Federation of Federal

Employees (NFFE), 144
National Labor Relations Act
    (NLRA), 26, 27, 28
    on hazardous conditions,
        99–100
    limitations, 92–93
    retaliation protections, 106
    Section 8 provisions, 90–92
    Weingarten Rights and, 104
National Labor Relations Board
    (NLRB), 33, 90–91, 92, 128,
    137
National Labor Relations Board v.
    Weingarten, Inc. (1975),
    130–131
National Maritime Union (NMU),
    144–145
National Right to Work
    Committee, 27
National Rural Letter Carriers'
    Association (NRLCA), 145
National Treasury Employees
    Union (NTEU), 19, 145
national union organizations,
    17–18, 30
negligence
    DFR and, 33
    workers' compensation laws
        and, 101
negotiations. *See* bargaining
new hires, two-tier pay systems
    and, 58–59
Newspaper Guild, 18
night work, 59
nomination, candidate, 37
non-negotiable bargaining, 52
non-union workers, 7, 9, 59, 61,
    110
North American Free Trade
    Agreement (NAFTA), 21
Northland Poster Collective, 137
notification of job reductions, 63,
    65
Novelty and Production Workers,
    International Union of Allied,
    145

O

Occupational Safety and Health Act (OSHA), 98–100, 129
Occupational Safety and Health Administration (OSHA), 98, 137
Office and Professional Employees International Union (OPEIU), 145
officers, union
    election of, 17, 38
    local, 17
    reporting requirements, government, 38
"on call" compensation, 59
OP+CMIA (Plasters' & Cement Masons' International Association of the US & Canada, Operative), 146
open shops, 28, 129
Operating Engineers, International Union of (IUOE), 145
Oregon School Employees Association (OSEA), 145
organizing, 109–110, 129
    immediate benefits, 110
    individual roles in, 114
    threats to, 111–112
    union density, 110–111
    violence and, 113
outside sales employees, 95
overtime, 59, 95

P

PACs, 114
pain and suffering relief
    grievances and, 74–75
    workers' compensation laws and, 101
Painters & Allied Trades of the US & Canada, International Brotherhood of (IBPAT), 146
Paper, Allied-Industrial, Chemical Employees International Union (PACE), 145–146
parental leave, 59

past practice, 59, 89, 129
pay. *See also* strike pay
    collective bargaining agreements on, 58–59
    conflicting negotiating interests over, 8
    discrimination in, 95–96
    inequality in, and union density, 111
    labor laws on, 94–95
    mandatory bargaining on, 51–52
    severance, 63
pensions, 51–52, 100–101
personal appearance standards, 64
personnel records, 64
Philippines, United Parcel Service strike (1997) and, 20
Plasters' & Cement Masons' International Association of the US & Canada, Operative (OP+CMIA), 146
Plate Printers, Die Stampers & Engravers Union of North America, 146
Police Associations, International Union of (IUPA), 146
political action committees (PACs), 114
political contributions, agency fees and, 28, 114
politics, 114–115
Postal Workers Union, American (APWU), 146
posters
    on FLSA rights, 95
    Northland Poster Collective, 137
    on OSHA rights and responsibilities, 98–99
Pregnancy Discrimination Act, 96
prevailing rate wages, 9
Pride at Work, 137–138
private sector, 3, 129. *See also* labor law
probationary periods, 63
problem identification, grievances

and, 70
Professional and Technical Engineers, International Federation of (IFPTE), 146
Professional Athletes, Federation of, 146
professional employees, FLSA and, 95
progressive discipline, 61
promotion discrimination, 96
public employees
    bargaining by, 48–49
    collective bargaining agreements for, 58
    discrimination against, 95
    FLRA protections for, 93
    interest-based bargaining and, 53
    organizing, 109
    politics and, 115
    state and local, 93–94
public relations campaigns, 50–51
public sector, 3, 129. *See also* labor law; public employees
punishment, for infractions, 61–62. *See also* discipline
punitive damages, grievances and, 74–75

Q

quality circles, 15

R

Radio Association, American (ARA), 146
Railway Labor Act, 93, 129
Randolph Institute. *See* A. Philip Randolph Institute
rank and file, 129. *See also* members/membership
ratification, contract, 129
    printing contracts after, 46–47
    voting on, 24, 45–46
receiverships, 39. *See also* trusteeships
record-keeping, grievances and, 70
"redcircling," 59, 129

reductions in force, 63, 65
regional union organizations, 17
Rehabilitation Act (1973), 96
rehiring priorities, 63
religion, union membership and, 27
reservists, military, 97–98
retaliation against workers, 111–113, 129
    protections against, 106–107
retiree benefits, permissive bargaining on, 52
retirement, phased, 63
retirement benefit plans
    collective bargaining agreements on, 63
    law on private plans, 100–101
retraining, 63
Reuther, Walter, 10
rights
    to bargaining information, 52
    Civil Rights Act (1964), Title VII, 95–96
    in disciplinary actions, 104
    ERISA, 100
    internal union, 37–39, 64
    of management, in grievances, 68
    OSHA, 98–99
    and responsibilities of members, 23–31
    union institutional, 64
    violations of union members', 35–37, 38–39
    voting, 24
    Weingarten (1975), 104
    workplace, 87, 88–89
"right to work" states, 28, 129
Rockefeller industrial empire, 113
Roofers, Waterproofers and Allied Workers, United Union of, 147

S

safety. See health and safety
schedules, work, 59
School Administrators, American

Federation of (AFSA), 147
Screen Actors Guild (SAG), 147
Seafarers International Union of North America (SIU), 147
Seeger, Pete, 5
seniority, 8, 130
Service Employees International Union (SEIU), 147
severance pay, 63
sex discrimination, 96
Sheet Metal Workers International Association (SMWIA), 147
shift differentials, 59, 95
sick leave, 59, 97
Signalmen, Brotherhood of Railroad (BRS), 147
smoking regulations, 64
social activities, 28
social justice, 9–10
Social Security system, 9
South Dakota State Employees Organization (SD-SEO), 147
speech, freedom of, 37–38
staff, union, 17
    dues support for, 24
    national, 18
    salaries and expenses of, 38
Stage Employees & Moving Picture Techs, Artists & Allied Crafts (IATSE), 148
stall tactics, employer, 112
state anti-discrimination laws, 96
State Employees Association of North Carolina, Inc. (SEANC), 148
Steelworkers of America, United (USWA), 148
stewards, 130
    chief, 16
    employee discipline and, 104
    questions for, 14–16
    role and selection of, 13–14
    time off to represent members, 64
strike pay, 47
strikes, 47–49, 130
    economic, 48

unfair labor practice, 48
United Parcel Service (1997), 20
Washington Post (1970s), 48
structure, union, 13–21, 89
substance abuse counseling services, 64
substantive rights, under ERISA, 100
supervisors
    grievance procedures and, 76
    NLRA exclusion of, 92
Supreme Court
    Beck decision (1988), 27
    on fair representation, 33
    Weingarten Rights (1975), 104
surveillance campaigns, union organizing and, 112
surveys, bargaining, 42–43

T

taxes
    fairness of, 25
    union dues and, 31
Teachers, American Federation of (AFT), 148
teachers, elementary and secondary, 95
team concept (of management), 15
Teamsters, International Brotherhood of (IBT), 13, 20, 148
technology, workplace, 48, 62, 65
tentative contract agreements, 45
termination, employee, 61
terms and conditions of employment, 8
"test case" grievances, 83–84
testimony, arbitration hearing, 81
tips from customers, 95
Title VII of Civil Rights Act (1964), 95–96
total quality management (TQM), 15
Train Dispatchers, American, 148
transfer opportunities, discrimination in, 96

Transit Union, Amalgamated (ATU), 148
Transportation • Communications International Union (TCU), 148–149
Transportation Union, United (UTU), 149
Transport Workers Union of America (TWU), 148
travel (work-related) compensation, 59
travel discounts, 8
trusteeships, 39, 130
two-tier pay systems, 58–59

U

UAW (Automobile, Aerospace & Agricultural Implement Workers of America), 111, 140
UBC (Carpenters & Joiners of America, United Brotherhood of), 141
UFCW (Food and Commercial Workers International Union, United), 142
UFW (Farm Workers of America, United), 141
UMWA (Mine Workers of America, United), 113, 144
undocumented workers, 93, 101
unemployment compensation benefits, 9, 47
unfair labor practices (ULPs), 48, 91, 130
Union Communication Services, Inc., 138
union contracts. *See* collective bargaining agreements
Union Jobs Clearinghouse, 138
Union Label Department, AFL-CIO, 138
union local, 130
    assessments, 30
    structural variations in, 16–17
    trusteeships on, 39
union meetings

for contract ratification, 45
participation in, 37, 89, 119
Union of Needletrades, Industrial and Textile Employees (UNITE), 18, 149
Union Privilege, 138
union stewards. *See* stewards
unions
    constitutions and bylaws, 89, 126
    defined, 5–11
    density of, 110
    dues, 28–31
    duty of fair representation (DFR), 33–35
    effect of wages on all workers, 9
    employee discipline and, 104
    grievance initiation by, 69
    institutional rights of, 64
    internal rights of, 37–39
    laws on membership in, 26–28
    members' rights and responsibilities, 10–11, 23–31
    operations of, 13–21
    organizing, 109–114
    reasonable rules of, 38
    responsibility to members, 33–39
    social justice and, 9–10
    staff, 17
    strike pay, 47
    workplace structure, 6
    workplace view, 13–16
union security, 23–26
union shop, 26, 130
union wage effect, 9
UNITE (Union of Needletrades, Industrial and Textile Employees), 18, 149
United Association of Plumbing and Pipefitting Industry (UA), 146
United Auto Workers (UAW), 111, 140
United Electrical, Radio and Machine Workers of America (UE), 19, 149

United Nations, International Labor Organization (ILO) and, 21
United Parcel Service strike (1997), 20
unwritten laws, workplace rights and, 88–89
USWA (Steelworkers of America, United), 148
Utah Public Employees' Association (UPEA), 149
Utah School Employees Association (USEA), 149
Utility Workers Union of America (USUA), 149
UTU (Transportation Union, United), 149

V

vacation leave, 59
voting requirements, 100
veterans, rights of, 97–98
violence against workers, 113
voluntary bargaining, 52
voting
    on contract ratification, 24, 45–46
    in union elections, 37, 38

W

wages. *See* pay (employee)
Wagner Act, 130. *See also* National Labor Relations Act
WARN laws, 97
Washington Post strike (1970s), 48
weekend work, 59
Weingarten Rights, 104–105, 130–131
Western Europe, United Parcel Service strike (1997) and, 20
whistleblowers, 100, 131
win-win bargaining, 52, 131. *See also* interest-based bargaining
Wisconsin, public employee protections in, 94
withdrawal card, honorable, 30
witnesses, arbitration hearing, 80,

81

women. *See* Coalition of Labor
Union Women
"work, then grieve" rule, 68
Worker Adjustment and Retraining
Notification Act (WARN,
1989), 97
workers' compensation, 101, 131
workplace
access by union representatives,
64
health and safety, 63, 98–100
legislation, 9
posters on FLSA rights, 95
posters on OSHA rights and
responsibilities, 98–99
relocation, 65
union vs. non-union structure,
6, 7
union committee structure,
16–17
view of union from, 13–16
workplace rights, 87–101. *See also*
labor law; rights
contracts, 87
employer handbooks and regulations, 88
government laws and regulations, 88
union constitutions and bylaws,
89
unwritten laws, 88–89
vigilance over, 89
work release, grievance procedures
and, 76
written records. *See* record-keeping